PURA VIDA

the

waterfalls

and

hot springs

of

costa rica

Production Notes:
Cover & text design by Grant Tatum
Cartography by Grant Tatum
Cover photo: Upper Santo Cristo by Sam Mitchell
Photographs by Sam Mitchell
Additional photography by Rafael and Marilyn Navarro Leiton

Library of Congress Cataloging-in-Publication Data

Mitchell, Sam
    Pura vida: the waterfalls and hot springs of Costa Rica
    p. cm.
    1. Hot springs–Costa Rica 2. Waterfalls–Costa Rica I. Title
    GB 1198.4.C8M57 1995
    917.286'045–dc20 94-44226 CIP

    ISBN 0-89732-172-3

Menasha Ridge Press
3169 Cahaba Heights Road
Birmingham, Alabama 35243

To my mother, Elaine Mitchell, who didn't yell at me too much when I ran ahead on the trails.

ACKNOWLEDGMENTS:

Muchas gracias to my friends who made this book possible, particularly:

Rafael and Marilyn Navarro Leiton, for providing several photos in this book, not to mention undying moral support;

Mi amiga, Karina Proctor, for her undying sense of adventure and love of laughter while I was researching this book;

Barbara Bowden, for her offers of food and shelter;

All the *ticos* and *ticas* who gave me directions the best they could, considering my abysmal Spanish;

Rina Lee, my ace computer wiz, for her ceaseless energy and encouragement. This book is as much a product of her perspiration as my inspiration.

Table of Contents

INTRODUCTION

ABOUT THIS BOOK

If you could see where I am sitting as I write these words, you would buy this little book. This I know, because in these pages are the secrets to discovering this little slice of tropical paradise, as well as dozens more.

Let me set the scene for you. It's the first day of winter, and I am lying naked on a slab of sun-warmed granite jutting out above a tropical waterfall in a little canyon deep in the jungles of Costa Rica. Layer upon layer of green on green softens the intensity of the noonday sun, which burns brilliantly in a sky the color of robins' eggs. The only sounds I hear are the never-ending lullaby of the cascading water, the lazy drone of katydids, and an occasional shriek or hoot from a passing parrot or monkey. My only slender connection to the real world (for surely *this* world is fantasy) is this pen in my hand. Well, you get the picture. . .

Over the course of four winters, I have spent more than a year seeking out magic spots such as this (a tough and dirty job, but someone's got to do it!). I realize how blessed I am to be able to live this lifestyle. I realize, too, that most people don't—or won't—allow themselves the time to enjoy a carefree existence. Their "vacation time" must be squeezed into a month, two weeks, or even less. This book is for those people.

If you're a lover of waterfalls, hot springs, and other wet and wild places, you've already made the most important decision to vacation in Costa Rica. Take a country roughly the size of Vermont and New Hampshire combined, fill it with a half-dozen mountain ranges (including a dozen or so active and sleeping volcanoes), then cover it with 100 to 300 inches of rain per year, and you have the recipe for a waterfall lover's paradise. A walk up almost any mountain stream should eventually lead to at least a small *catarata*. By far the most difficult thing about writing this book was not wondering what to include but what to leave out.

I will assume that you have already purchased and perused one of the many general guidebooks to Costa Rica, so I will not waste words repeating information easily found elsewhere. There are, however, a few pointers germane to Costa Rican waterfalls and hot springs in general—and this book in particular—that bear mentioning before we get into the nitty-gritty of how to discover the *pura vida* in the wilds of Costa Rica.

ABOUT THE AUTHOR

I'll announce from the get-go that I have never written a guidebook (or any book, for that matter), and it probably shows. My sole intention in writing this book is to tell others about places I have discovered—on and off the beaten track—and to offer the best advice I can to help others get there.

If you're an engineer, an accountant, or other stickler for detail, you may not like my style. And you will *hate* the laid-back style of most Costa Ricans, who couldn't care less about the difference between an inch and a mile, a minute and an hour, because you'll reach a waterfall sooner or later if you keep walking upstream.

I *have* worked hard to keep a sharp eye out for landmarks and changes in trail direction, and to report them accurately, to keep you from getting lost too many times. I can't tell you exactly how tall the falls are once you get there because I have no way of measuring them. But I can report (even accurately in some cases!) the most important item for any self-respecting hedonist—the water temperature!

My only true qualification is a genuine love of my subject matter, and a genuine desire to share my joyful discoveries with others who will share that joy, while leaving nothing behind but their footsteps.

ABOUT THE WEATHER

The two main things affecting Costa Rica's weather—and therefore her waterfalls—are season (wet and dry) and altitude.

To oversimplify Costa Rica's weather, it rains *a lot* from April to November, which is why I choose to visit Costa Rica between November and April. I've never visited Costa Rica during the rainy season, but common sense (not to mention logjams and flotsam high in riparian trees) tells me that the trails mentioned in this book would be sloppy at best, and possibly life-threatening where they cross the river channels. On the flip-side, many of the smaller falls—particularly along the dry Pacific Coast—can slow to a trickle by February, and water quality can suffer. As in any wilderness outing, use common sense and caution, and double-check with the locals if you have concerns about safety.

Costa Rica's altitude—ranging from sea level to more than 12,000 feet in less than 100 miles—is the main indicator of water temperature. While stream temperatures may reach 80° F. (26.5° C.) along the hot Pacific Coast, streams above 4,000 feet or so are generally too chilly to swim in comfortably. This means that the majority of the country's most spectacular cascades are best enjoyed from the riverbanks. Fortunately, benevolent Mother Nature has smiled warmly on the chilly volcanic mountain ranges and dappled them with warm and hot springs. Until you've splashed back and forth, otter-like, between a cold rushing mountain stream and a soothing 100° F. (38°C.) hot spring high in the Costa Rican cloud forest, you haven't earned your true hedonist stripes.

WHAT TO PACK

Again, I'm not going to waste words repeating the other guidebooks, but here is my "essential list" for a first-class waterfall visit:

Day trips: Lightweight but sturdy walking shoes; high-quality air mattress (for reclining on rocks and floating in pools); drinks; biodegradable soap; flashlight (just in case); book to read.

Overnight trips: Warm clothes (long pants and sweater) for altitudes over 3,000 feet (1,000 meters); tent; mosquito repellent; lighter; flashlight; sleeping bag. For coastal areas, make a lightweight sleeping bag by folding a large cotton sheet in half lengthwise and stitching along the side and bottom.

ABOUT TRANSPORTATION

In my travels around Costa Rica, I've been blessed with the use of my own car, which I drive down from the States each year (not nearly the hassle one would expect, and the option I'd highly recommend if you're planning to stay for any length of time). I admit to those without cars that it can be easier said than done—but not impossible—to reach some of the more remote falls.

If you don't have the luxury of a private vehicle, you're left with two choices: rental cars or buses. Fortunately, rental cars are relatively easy to obtain *if you have a credit card*, but can be quite pricey (up to $400 per week in 1994). Also, I have heard horror stories from fellow gringos who have been hit with exorbitant damage charges for minor dings and scratches their cars suffered on Costa Rica's less-than-perfect roadways.

For all the suffering they inflict upon passengers and other drivers, Costa Rica's buses do an amazing job of moving people to even the most remote mountain-top villages. You'll rarely be more than a few miles from the nearest bus stop. Getting from the last bus stop to the trailheads can be tricky; if you can't score a "taxi" or hitchhike, do as most Costa Ricans do—hoof it.

ABOUT ACCOMMODATIONS

As it is my conviction that the Costa Rican wilderness experience can only be truly served by sleeping under the stars, I have geared this book toward camping. I have tried to point out the best campsites at or near the falls and springs, but sometimes topography dictates that you do the best you can. For those who don't like sharing their hammocks with tarantulas, scorpions, and vampire bats, you can nearly always find some sort of hotel in the town closest to the falls. However, if you're looking for a true hotel and restaurant guide, you should turn to one of the many general guidebooks available.

ABOUT CAMPING

Of all the things in the world I am not, "Costa Rican lawyer" would have to rate right up near the top of the list. I'll never make sense of their laws, but I *believe* this is a true fact: The *waters* of Costa Rica (including rivers, lakes, and beaches) are public, but the *land* around the waters is private. Therefore, unless you're a duck, you're going to have a pretty tough time camping at Costa Rican waterfalls without trespassing.

That's the bad news; the

good news is—in my experience, at least—nobody seems to care. Once again, use good sense and common courtesy; don't trash the place or burn it down, and you should be okay. If someone threatens to kick you out, offer a small sum of money. If that doesn't work, leave quietly.

One unfortunate but inevitable result of increased "ecotourism" is the increasing popularity of "land crossing fees," usually running from $3 to $5. What can I say? Grin and bear it.

Ironically, a more serious problem is the difficulty of camping on *public* lands—particularly in the national parks, where many of the falls in this book are located. Many of these parks are closed entirely to camping, and the ones that are open often cram people into tiny little campgrounds by squawking rangers' radios.

Note: As of January, 1995, the short-sighted bureaucrats began charging $15 per *day*, per *person*, to visit any national park in Costa Rica! This ridiculous policy affects the following destinations: Hidden Falls, Congrejo Falls, Hitoy-Cerere Falls, Tapanti (Salto and Palmitos Falls), San Pedrillo Falls, Playa Llorona falls, and Rincon de la Vieja hot springs. They're still beautiful places but budget-minded tourists beware.

ABOUT LITTERING

In a word: DON'T. Your mama doesn't live in the Costa Rican jungle. Pack it in, pack it out.

And please, folks, use a little common sense and common courtesy when answering nature's call in the forest—particularly near streams that may be someone's drinking water source. If you can't *bury* your offering to Mother Nature (the best option), at least *cover* it with a rock or log. (And watch out for tarantulas!)

ABOUT GETTING LOST

Finding one's way in Costa Rica, particularly if you don't speak Spanish (as I still don't after four winters there), is the most common headache you will encounter when looking for these places. You will usually find fellow gringos in the more popular spots, but there are fewer English–speaking Costa Ricans than you might think.

There are two main reasons

for the headaches. For one thing, it does very little good to know how to ask directions if you can't understand the answer. For another, *ticos* and *ticas* (the nickname for Costa Rican men and women) in all likelihood will not know the answer—particularly because most are not wilderness lovers as a general rule—but they may be embarrassed that they don't know and give you wrong information.

The trick to asking directions in Costa Rica is to learn a few phrases, then ask *closed-ended* questions (yes or no, approximate distances and times, which direction, etc.). Don't start by asking where (*donde*) something is: ask the person if he knows where (*sabe*, pronounced SAH-bay) a place is. Once you think you have some vague idea what the person is saying, double-check by asking if he or she is sure (*seguro*) the information is correct.

Here is a sample of the classic conversation I had approximately 10,000 times while writing this book:

Me: "*¿Por favor, sabe Usted donde está la catarata (o agua termales) acerca de aqui?*" ("Excuse me, do you know where the waterfall [or hot spring] near here is?")

Tico: "*No se.*" ("I don't know.")

Or, more commonly, a blank-to-terrified stare like someone would have if being interrogated by an alien from the Red Planet. After a few tries, I would finally find someone who knew (or, more likely, pretended to know) what I was talking about. At that point, I'd receive an answer that sounded like *I* was interrogating an alien from the Red Planet. In other words, an unintelligible barrage of Spanish. This is the point where I would begin the closed-ended questions.

Me: "*Lo siento, mi español es muy terrible. ¿Bien, este es el camino (o sendero) a la cascada, si o no?*" ("I'm sorry, my Spanish is very terrible. Okay, is this the road [or the path] to the waterfall, yes or no?")

Tico: "*Si.*"

(Okay, I know I'm dreaming here. Nine out of ten times, the answer will be no, at which time you have my condolences. At some point, you will get to this point, I promise.)

Me: "*Fantastico. ¿Bien, cuanto kilometros mas o menos?*" ("Fantastic. Okay, how many kilometers more or less?") (A kilometer is roughly five-eights of a mile.)

Tico: "*Tres, cuatro.*" ("Three or four.") This will be followed by a long string of unintelligible Spanish jabber.

Me: "*¿Cuantos minutos?*" ("How many minutes?")

Tico: "*Diez, quince.*" ("Ten, fifteen.") More jabber.

Me: "*¿Está Usted seguro?*" ("Are you sure?")

Tico: "*Si.*" (Yeah, right. . .)

Me: "*¿En qué direccion está el sendero, izquierda o derecha?*" ("In which direction is the trail, left or right?")

Tico: "*Derecha.*" ("Right.") Extreme caution here: *Derecha* is Spanish for "right," while *directa* is Spanish for "straight ahead." Listen extremely carefully.

Me: "*¿Hay un rotulo a la catarata?*" ("Is there a sign to the falls?")

Tico: "*No.*" ("Where do you think you are, Yosemite?")

Me: "*Muchas gracias.*" ("Thank you.")

Tico: "*Mucho gusto.*" (Literally, "with much pleasure," the Costa Rican colloquialism for "you're welcome.")

This final exchange will doubtless end with one last barrage of unintelligible jabber that usually means something like this: "You do know, you stupid gringo, that the waterfall dried up three years ago and all you'll find there now is a nest of rabid vampire bats and the skeletons of other dumb tourists who were attacked by killer bees."

One serious note: If you ever do really get lost in the forest (whether you're in Costa Rica or the U.S.), the safest and quickest way back to civilization is to follow any stream *downstream* (that's downhill!) until you reach a house or a bridge. Even if it takes you two days, you'll at least have water to drink.

ABOUT GUIDES

The best and easiest way to avoid getting lost while looking for any of the waterfalls in this book would be to hire a local guide to lead you there. The obvious advantages of hiring a guide are safety and convenience, while the obvious disadvantage is expense. The going rate was about $35 per person in 1994.

A not-so-obvious disadvantage—and the reason Yours Truly elected not to employ guides while exploring the places in this book—is the damage guides can do to what I call the "Tarzan quotient" of these beautiful spots.

Chalk it up to male ego or gringo arrogance, I simply enjoy the rush of "discovering" new and exotic places on my own. And once I'm there, I like to have the freedom and privacy to *act* like Tarzan (or, better yet, Tarzan and Jane!), a freedom that would be curtailed by the presence of a stranger.

The choice is yours and should depend a lot on your "comfort level" of being alone in the jungle in some distant, exotic land. Getting lost in the jungle, especially as darkness approaches before 6:00 P.M., can be a terrifying experience. Particularly around "ecotourist" destinations such as Montezuma, Rincon de la Vieja, Monteverde, Fortuna, and Dominical, it's easy to find knowledgeable guides to take you to the falls on foot, or, more commonly, on horseback—but you'll pay the price for their knowledge.

In more remote locations—and in the "hot spots" too, for that matter—you can always ask around and hire almost any teenaged *muchacho* to lead you to the falls for a fraction of the cost you'd pay a professional outfit. Best of all, you can politely shoo him away when you and Jane get there, and find your own way back later.

ABOUT THE METRIC SYSTEM

The confusion I suffer as a gringo from the United States traveling in a metric system land will be apparent throughout this book as I freely travel back and forth between the two systems in my descriptions of distances. Do not fret; it's *really* not that confusing. Here are the general (not exact) rules to keep in mind when going back and forth between the two systems:

➤ A meter (39 inches) is roughly equivalent to a yard (36 inches). To convert distances in feet to distances in meters, divide by three; to convert distances in meters to distances in feet, multiply by three—not perfect, but close enough for government work and waterfall-hopping.

➤ A kilometer (1,000 meters) is roughly .6 miles.

➤ A mile is roughly 1.6 kilometers.

Here are a few other handy references:

➤ One meter = 100 centimeters = 39.37 inches = 3.28 feet.

➤ One yard = 3 feet = 36 inches = 0.914 meters.

➤ One kilometer = 1,000 meters = 0.621 miles.

➤ Five kilometers = 3.1 miles.

➤ Ten kilometers = 6.2 miles.

➤ Five miles = 8kilometers.

➤ Ten miles = 16 kilometers.

➤ 50 feet = 15.24 meters.

➤ 100 feet = 30.48 meters.

➤ 15 meters = 48.8 feet.

➤ 30 meters = 97.5 feet.

You'll pick up linear distances pretty easily, but things get a lot tougher in the Celsius-to-Fahrenheit temperature conversions. The blame for this falls squarely on gringos from the United States.

Besides supporting an obese war machine with our hard-earned tax dollars, the strangest thing "Americans" do as a collective group is to use a temperature gauge in which freezing is 32 degrees above zero. Don't ask me why (I think it has something to do with a ploy to keep Vikings from sacking Miami), but it's not going to change without an act of Congress—and *I'm* certainly not going to vote for anyone who says my blood temperature is 37 degrees!

Fortunately, there's hope. There's a Celsius-to-Fahrenheit conversion equation whereby you multiply the cube root of the future value of Costa Rican peccary bellies by the hypotenuse of the Bermuda Triangle, bake in a warm oven until golden brown, and add 32. To convert from Fahrenheit to Celsius, simply reverse the process, or look at any 79¢ thermometer with both scales on it, which is what I did to come up with this table that

FAHRENHEIT/CELSIUS CONVERSON TABLE

C.	F.	C.	F.	C.	F.	C.	F.
15°	60°	23°	74°	30°	86°	38°	100°
16°	61°	24°	75°	31°	88°	39°	102°
17°	63°	25°	77°	32°	90°	40°	104°
18°	65°	26°	79°	33°	91°	41°	106°
19°	66°	27°	81°	34°	93°	42°	108°
20°	68°	28°	83°	35°	95°	43°	110°
21°	70°	29°	84°	36°	97°	44°	111°
22°	72°			37°	98°		

should cover all the water temperatures you will encounter in the waterfalls and hot springs in this book.

ABOUT NUDITY

One of my few complaints about Costa Rica is the country's almost Draconian view toward nudity, including toplessness for women. In a country where the average bikini wouldn't cover a tangerine, the anti-nudity bias can cause the hedonist tourist a problem. Basically, nudity—including bare breasts—is strictly prohibited everywhere in the country. Two minor exceptions are Montezuma and Puerto Viejo, where topless sunbathing seems to be at least tolerated.

Over the years, I've worked out this seemingly acceptable (but technically illegal) compromise: if the waterfall or hot spring is isolated—as are most in this book—I will generally go nude if I'm by myself or with other gringo tourists (gringos include Europeans and Canadians). If there are native Costa Ricans there when I arrive, it's a judgment call; *no* if small kids or elderly women are present, *perhaps* if it's a young adult crowd. If I'm there first and

Costa Ricans arrive, again it's a judgment call. One compromise that covers the "bare essentials" is a loincloth made of two bandanas tied together.

One unfortunate exception: if you're a woman traveling alone—or even a small group of women without male friends—cover up. Cover everything up: a sexist, sad-but-true comment. Bottom line: use common sense and good judgment.

ABOUT MY SELECTIONS

When I first started this book, my plan was to write about the most beautiful waterfalls in Costa Rica, period. If you needed a helicopter, Sherpa guides, and a six-week supply of freeze-dried rations to *get* to them, that was your problem, not mine.

Then I realized that, while such a book might be okay for National Geographic photographers and Indiana Jones, it probably wouldn't do much for the average tourist of average physical ability with limited time and a moderate budget. With my audience more in focus (not that you're average), I produced this

10

list of twenty-nine waterfalls and seven hot springs.

My list covers the widest range of experience possible—from two-minute strolls to day-long, muscle-wrenching workouts—but it consistently tries to aim for the natural and the beautiful. And in Costa Rica, you never have to travel far to fill that bill. Each one of these places can be visited in a day or two, and many can be reached from downtown San José within a couple of hours.

I've attempted to rate these day trips on four levels of difficulty: easy, moderate, difficult, and arduous. These are, of course, subjective words coming from a physically active and in-shape male in his early thirties who has been exploring waterfalls since he was five. I know how to cross a mountain stream without falling, and how to tell a slippery rock from a safe one *before* I step on it. I grew up in the Deep South and am use to climbing hills in 95° F. (36° C.) heat and 95 percent humidity. If our descriptions and life experience don't match, chances are our definitions of the words "easy walk" may not, either.

Here is a thumbnail sketch of my definitions:

➤ **E A S Y :**

If you can't make this walk, you shouldn't buy this book, and you probably shouldn't be in Costa Rica on vacation. I suggest a condo in Cozumel, where the waiter can bring burritos and beer to your poolside chaise.

➤ **M O D E R A T E :**

You'll probably break into a healthy sweat on this walk, but if you're between the ages of 10 and 60 and can hold out for seven innings of softball, you'll do just fine.

➤ **D I F F I C U L T :**

Leave the kids, Grandma, and anyone who wears eye-shadow at home. You're going to skin your knees on this walk, and probably fall down a couple of times, but you'll have a good story to tell your lazy bum friends when you get back.

➤ **A R D U O U S :**

If you're between the ages of 20 and 25, have a death wish, can bench press 380 pounds, enjoy swinging through the trees like a chimpanzee, and don't mind the sight of blood (yours, that is), you'll have a blast!

In all seriousness, I would

Conditions — Hot Springs	OKAY FOR CHILDREN	EASY HIKE	MODERATE HIKE	DIFFICULT HIKE	ARDUOUS HIKE	LESS THAN A ONE-HOUR WALK EACH WAY	TRAIL WITHIN TWO MILES (3 KILOMETERS) OF BUS STOP	POSSIBLE DAY TRIP FROM SAN JOSÉ	CAMPING WITHIN TEN MINUTES *	SWIMMING POOL	BATHING POOL	CLOTHING OPTIONAL (IN MY OPINION-TECHNICALLY ILLEGAL)	WATER TEMPERATURE OVER 70°F (22°C)	MORE THAN 100 FEET (30 METERS) IN HEIGHT
A Rincon de la Vieja	●		●							●	●	●	●	●
B Rio Tabacon	●	●				●	●	●			●		●	
C Arenal	●	●				●	●	●		●	●		●	
D Orosi	●	●				●	●	●	●				●	
E Los Patios	●	●				●	●	●	●				●	
F Herradura	●	●				●					●	●	●	
G Rivas	●	●				●				●	●		●	

● yes

never steer somebody somewhere I felt was unsafe. In four winters of tromping around the wilds of Costa Rica—naked much of the time and barefoot all the time— the most serious injury I've ever received was a cut toe while walking across an open grassy field. At the same time, these aren't Sunday afternoon strolls in the park. See how you feel about a couple of the easy ones, and work your way up to bigger adventures.

IN A NUTSHELL

Before diving into the body of this book, I want to offer a quick summary of the waterfalls and hot springs I have covered. Following is a list of traits that should give you a fair summary of what to expect there. After the list of descriptive traits, I have listed the waterfalls and hot springs as they appear in order in this book.

HOW THIS BOOK IS ORGANIZED

This book is divided into two parts: waterfalls first, hot springs next. Each section takes you on a "tour" of Costa Rica, beginning in Montezuma (at the southern tip of the Nicoya Peninsula in northwest Costa Rica), then traveling in a roughly clockwise direction around the country, and ending on the southwest coast below Jaco Beach. In the first section, I will note if there is

Legend:

- ● yes
- ○ possibly
- ▲ see page 4 on camping

#	Waterfalls	OKAY FOR CHILDREN	EASY HIKE	MODERATE HIKE	DIFFICULT HIKE	ARDUOUS HIKE	LESS THAN A ONE-HOUR WALK EACH WAY	TRAIL WITHIN TWO MILES (3 KILOMETERS) OF BUS STOP	POSSIBLE DAY TRIP FROM SAN JOSÉ	CAMPING WITHIN TEN MINUTES	SWIMMING POOL	BATHING POOL	CLOTHING OPTIONAL (IN MY OPINION - TECHNICALLY ILLEGAL)	WATER TEMPERATURE OVER 70°F (22°C)	MORE THAN 100 FEET (30 METERS) IN HEIGHT
1	Montezuma	●		●			●	●		●	●			●	●
2	Tambor			●				●		●		●		●	
3	Hidden Falls				●					▲	●		●	●	
4	Congrejo	●		●						▲	●		●	●	○
5	Libano	●	●				●	○		●	●	●	●	●	
6	Monteverde					●									●
7	Fortuna	●		●				○	●	●	●	●			●
8	Chorros	●	●				●		●	●					●
9	La Paz	●	●				●	●	●	●					○
10	San Fernando	●	●			●			●	●			●		●
11	Cariblanco			●			●		●	●					●
12	Angel/Congo	●		●			●	●	●	●	●				●
13	Toro Amarillo		●				●		●	●					●
14	Laguna Kopper	●	●				●	●		●	●			●	
15	Turrialba	●	●				●		●		●	●			
16	Hitoy-Cerere			●						▲	●	●	●	●	●
17	Salto					●				▲					●
18	Palmitos				●					▲		●			
19	Savegre/San Gerardo			●		●				●	●	●			
20	Diamante			●			●				●	●		●	
21	Santo Cristo	●		●			●	○		●	●		○	●	●
22	Dominicalito	●	●				●		●	●	●		○	●	
23	Rio Catarata	●	●				●			●	●		●	●	
24	Puerto Nuevo	●		●			●			●	●		●	●	
25	Palma Norte	●	●				●	●		●	●		○	●	
26	San Pedrillo			●			●			▲		●	●	●	
27	Playa Llorona				●					▲		●	●	●	
28	Hatillo	●	●				●	●		●	●	●		●	
29	Pozo Azul	●	●				●			●	●	●		●	

a hot spring in the same vicinity. (For example, after discussing the waterfalls in Rincon de la Vieja National Park, I will refer you to the hot springs in the second sec-tion.)

Okay, shall we begin our journey?

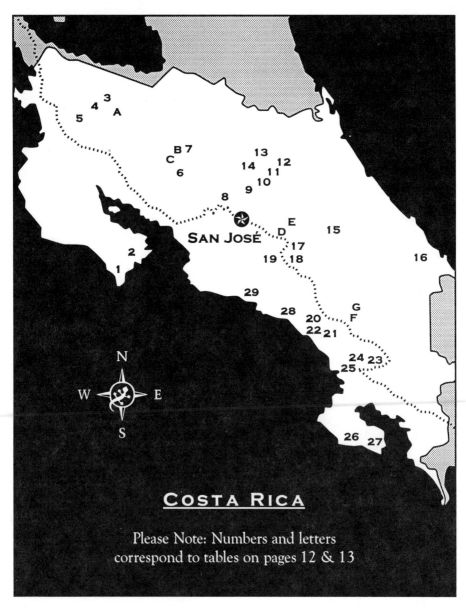

COSTA RICA

Please Note: Numbers and letters correspond to tables on pages 12 & 13

MONTEZUMA FALLS

INTRODUCTION

I'm leery of opening this book in Montezuma for two reasons.

For one thing, once you've discovered this little slice of heaven in a hidden corner of earth, you'll have no motivation to explore the other places in the book. More importantly, my expatriate gringo friends in Montezuma have threatened to feed me to the crocodiles if I bring even one more tourist there. While I share their feelings, the sad truth is that the Montezuma secret is out (as evidenced by the "Hotel from Hell" festering like a canker sore in Playa Tambor, 15 miles away). So, a few more casual travelers may as well enjoy it while they can before the party ends in a couple more years.

For my tastes, Montezuma is the perfect heady combination of scenery, beaches, and nightlife, making it one of my favorite spots in all of Costa Rica. To top it off, it is a waterfall lover's paradise. Fresh water is abundant, and almost any stream will soon lead to a waterfall. Water temperature approaches 80° F. (26.5° C.), and most of the small streams are private enough for nude sunbathing.

The queen of waterfalls (the largest by far and therefore the most popular) is on Rio Montezuma, a moderate 20-minute walk south, toward Cabo Blanco National Park from the village.

The falls are actually a series of three cascades that get progressively larger as they plunge downriver, ending in a magnificent cascade of approximately 90 to 100 feet. The swimming hole at the bottom, roughly 80 feet in diameter, is the stuff winter-weary gringos' dreams are made of. Before the dry season arrives in mid-January, the jungle is lush around the falls, and wildlife is abundant. The vast majority of tourists congregate in the pool at the bottom of the lower falls, and it can get crowded, especially around Christmas.

To truly savor the Montezuma experience, I highly recommend the short, but difficult, climb to the upper falls. All your sweating and moaning will be worth it the moment you try the Tarzan swing and crash into the uppermost swimming hole. You can spend the day lolling around the warm rocks that separate the two upper falls. Or, if you're really brave—or crazy—you can high-dive off the 40-foot middle falls into the small diving hole atop the main falls.

However you choose to spend your time at Montezuma Falls, you will have enjoyed one of the quintessential Costa Rican waterfall experiences.

DIRECTIONS

Getting to Montezuma, on the southern tip of the Nicoya Peninsula in northwest Costa Rica, is, unfortunately, much easier than it was a couple of years ago, but it's still quite an adventure. If you're driving, take the car ferry from Puntarenas to Tambor, then drive south for approximately one hour. If you're on foot, take the passenger ferry to Paquera, and a bus will be waiting there to take you to Montezuma.

The well-beaten trail to the falls begins at the fence on the south bank of the river, immediately past the bridge and restaurant, a five-minute walk south of the village. Follow the easy trail along the left bank of the river to the top of the cataracts (approximately five minutes), then carefully cross the river above the cataracts to the right bank.

The trail, now much smaller,

hugs the right bank for 150 to 300 feet, then splits—one way continues to hug the river shore, the other veers off into the woods. Either way is okay, but I prefer the forest route. In a few minutes, the trail returns to the riverside, and the final approach to the main falls along the right river bank can be a little tricky. Be careful of slippery rocks.

You will reach the main falls 20 to 30 minutes from the time you leave the village. While the falls are beautiful, the true jungle explorer will no doubt want to continue to the more remote upper falls. To reach the top, continue along the right side of the pool, and look for the almost vertical path, which veers off to the right up a steep hill just before the little side stream enters from the right. Huff and puff your way up the steep path using roots and trees for hand-holds. The trail will level out as you enter the woods. Cross the small side stream, cross a small meadow, and head back into the woods.

After passing through the meadow, the trail appears to divide. The left fork goes to an overlook. The right (uphill) fork continues into the forest, then crosses a rather steep little gulch.

The final approach to the upper falls can be a little harrowing, especially if you're carrying a day pack. The trail plunges down a near-vertical drop and ends at a table of granite separating the two upper falls and pools.

PUNTA TAMBOR FALLS

INTRODUCTION

Montezuma Falls provides the perfect introduction to the joys of Costa Rica's waterfalls, but the true waterfall aficionado will not be able to rest until he or she has sampled the sensual delights of Punta Tambor Falls, a 3.5-mile walk along the beach to the north.

While not so spectacular as Montezuma Falls in size or grandeur, Punta Tambor Falls is a must-see for any hedonist because the warm water there plunges over a cliff directly into the ocean below. At high tide, you can soak your feet in saltwater while shampooing your hair in fresh.

The two-hour hike to the falls is nothing short of awe-inspiring, but there are a couple of drawbacks to keep in mind. The sun can be merciless, so try not to be on the beach between 10:00 A.M. and 2:00 P.M., and carry plenty of drinks. High tide can be uncomfortable at best, life-threatening at worst, so aim your walk for low tide.

All your efforts will be rewarded, however, the moment you slip under the pounding shower of the falls. Sitting on the little granite ledge at the bottom of Punta Tambor Falls, whitewater drumming against your head and shoulders and swirling around your waist and legs, ocean waves colliding against the rocks below, the aqua Pacific arching southward to the blue and green hills behind Montezuma. . . *This is pura vida* in its purest form, truly one of your vacation's pivotal moments. If you did nothing else on your trip to Costa Rica, this moment alone would be worth the price of the air fare.

DIRECTIONS

Head north (away from Cabo Blanco) from "downtown" Montezuma. Cross the first beach, approximately a half mile long. Just beyond the bungalows on your left, the path leaves the sand for a few minutes. When you emerge onto a small beach with a creek running through it, you'll find one of the nicest campsites in Costa Rica on the north side of the creek. You can follow this creek upstream for a few minutes to some nice small falls and a swimming hole.

The trail continues uphill and away from the sea for 500 yards or so, then passes some small houses before emptying onto a small rocky (but trashed-out) beach. There are some nice shady camping areas under the almond trees, but there is no fresh water and the sheer volume of garbage detracts from the experience.

In a few more meters, the trail passes by a small freshwater lagoon on your left, and empties onto the appropriately-named Playa Grande. Except for the omnipresent tons of plastic flot-sam and jetsam, I would rate this beach with the best of Costa Rica's, especially in terms of privacy. There are only a couple of houses at each end of the half-mile long beach, so nude sunbathing should be okay here—with discretion, of course.

You should have little trouble carving a campsite out of the almond trees. The main drawback to this beach is the absence of shade, particularly at high tide dur-

ing mid-day. Schedule your hike to the falls to miss Playa Grande at high tide, or between the hours of 10:00 A.M. and 4:00 P.M.

At the north end of Playa Grande, the trail can get tricky to follow. While it's possible to stick to the ocean at extreme low tide, I find it preferable to follow the jeep trail that leads inland and uphill to your left. The trail forks in about 300 feet. Stay to your right, and head downhill past a little house, until you arrive again at the seaside trail.

The trail skirts the top of some rocks, then leads to your third and final beach, a kilometer-long crescent-shaped beach. If you look carefully toward the north horizon, to the right and below the little pyramid-shaped hill in front of you, you can see the falls pouring off a ledge into the sea.

If you forgot to pack drinks for your trip, stop at the house nestled in a grove of coconut palms for a soul-restoring drink of *agua de pipa* from the trees. Toward the north end of the beach, about 300 feet shy of the falls, you will pass a freshwater lagoon (I understand it is fed by an underwater hot spring, but I've been unable to confirm this). The few almendra trees on the narrow sand bluff above the high tide line provide about the only shade for camping or picnicking near the falls.

It can be tough reaching the falls (particularly at high tide), and the rocks surrounding the cascade are extremely slippery and sharp, so use extreme caution. As I said, all your troubles will be forgotten the moment you plunge into the 78° F. (25° C.) water below the 30-foot falls.

While I highly recommend the walk from Montezuma as one of the prettiest beach treks in Costa Rica, there is a much quicker and easier "back door" to the falls. A luxury hotel, the Tango Mar (reached by car via the road back to Paquera) sits barely five minutes above the falls in all its gringo opulence. I've never been there, but it looks spendy.

RINCON DE LA VIEJA NATIONAL PARK

INTRODUCTION

In 1992, I probably would have called Rincon de la Vieja National Park, in the state of Guanacaste north of Liberia, Costa Rica's best-kept national secret. By now, I regret to report, the secret is out. Nonetheless, this jewel in Costa Rica's national park system still offers a relatively uncrowded mecca for the lover of wild places. Nestled on the slopes of a double volcano, the park offers cloud forests, alpine lakes, boiling mud pots, hot springs, and—of course—a myriad of beautiful falls.

All this exotic natural beauty does not come cheap, however, particularly for the budget-minded traveler. The two lodges at the border of the park are nice, but pricey, and the food is expensive. I highly recommend packing in your food and camping, but there's a small catch there, as well: there are no public buses to the volcano, and in the winter of 1993, a round-trip taxi fare from Liberia was $60. The best I can advise you is to try to bum a ride from a fellow gringo in Liberia.

The payoff for your trouble comes when you arrive. Due to the relative difficulty of reaching Rincon de la Vieja, the crowds are small, and the people there really want to be there (meaning no gobs of beer-guzzling yahoos with squawking radios and gangs of little kids). There is plenty of room to escape on the miles and miles of developed trails, and a hike up any of the thirty-two streams that drain off the volcano will quickly find you swallowed up in a true jungle experience. Trails are generally well-marked and easy to follow, but guides are available to take you to the hidden places.

The biggest bummer about Rincon de la Vieja is the fact that camping is limited to two small developed campgrounds, one near each of the ranger stations. While they are nice for what they are (a couple of dollars per night to pitch a tent), some of the true wilderness experience is lost.

DIRECTIONS

Once you've lined up transportation (you can always *walk*) from Liberia, the next trick is finding the place. First warning: DO NOT follow the signs to the park from downtown Liberia; that road will take you to the ranger station and campground

on the east side of the volcano. This is a nice enough spot, but what you want is the ranger station on the west slope.

To get there, head west on the Pan-American Highway, as if you were going to the Nicaraguan border. In approximately 3 miles, you will see a sign on your right pointing to the Rincon de la Vieja Lodge. (If you cross a bridge over the Rio Colorado, you have gone too far.) Turn right onto to this dirt road, and head up into the hills. After passing through a small village (bear right here), you will be charged a small toll at the gate. Beyond the gate the road forks, each way taking you to a hotel. Bear left here.

In a couple of miles, the road divides again. To reach the hot springs turn right toward the lodge; to reach the waterfalls, continue straight uphill toward the ranger station (the road's a lit-tle rough, but you'll be fine).

While the small campground below the ranger station could hardly be labeled a true wilder-ness experience, it makes a good base for journeys into the park. An excellent way to introduce yourself to the wonders of Rincon de la Vieja is to walk the easy-to-moderate, hour-long loop trail to the mud pots, steam vents, and nearby waterfall.

Heading east (away from the ranger station) you will immediately cross the Rio Colorado. In a couple of minutes, bear right at the fork in the trail, away from the catarata. The trail passes through an oak grove, then enters a wide open meadow thick with the aroma of sulfur.

In a few minutes, a trail will cut left toward the *fumarillos* (steam vents). Continue straight here, following the sign toward the *paillas* (mud pots). When the trail splits again, stay to your right, toward the *paillas* (the left fork leads to the lodge, and ultimately to the hot springs). In about five minutes, you will arrive at the fascinating—and potentially deadly—natural vats of boiling, oozing, blue-grey mud.

To return to the loop trail, work your way back to the turn-off to the *fumarillos*, which of course will now be a right turn. The trail will cut between some smaller (but still dangerous) mud pots, then appear to end at a small hot-water stream. You must work your way across this stream, then head uphill through the underbrush for a few meters, at which point you'll arrive at a gaping hole in the earth with steam boiling out of it.

The faint trail turns left at this steam vent and heads into the forest, roughly following the right bank of the creek upstream. You will pass another huge hissing steam vent, then arrive at a boiling hot spring, obviously much too hot for bathing.

If you look *very carefully*, you will pick out the trail continuing uphill to your right. The path re-enters the cloud forest and, after one tiny stream crossing, arrives at a pretty rushing mountain stream. A lovely 90-foot waterfall, which can range from delicate to awe-inspiring, depending on water level, erupts from the cloud forest two minutes up this stream. You can take a refreshing dip in the cold pool at the bottom, but it's too small for swimming.

The main loop trail—marked clearly and easy to follow by this point—leads up and over a couple of thickly forested hills, passing one of the biggest trees I've ever seen in Costa Rica. Turn right at the fork in the trail, and you will be back home in a couple of minutes.

Hidden Falls

INTRODUCTION

The best named waterfalls in all of Costa Rica are Cataratas Escondidas, or Hidden Falls—boy, is *that* an understatement! Three times I started out to the falls, and three times I failed. My fourth time up the volcano was my charm—and what a charm it was!

At about 40 feet (there are two much higher, inaccessible falls downstream), Upper Catarata Escondida can't be measured in terms of sheer grandeur. Its essence is much more intimate: a plume of water cascading through a small natural amphitheater of lush tropical vegetation and stone outcroppings, that lands in a topaz-green pool about 30 feet in diameter.

The crystal clear water is excellent for a refreshing dip if you schedule your visit for midday, when dappled sunshine warms the boulders that ring the pool. Indeed, the whole effect is so enchanting you'd almost think it was a Hollywood creation—until you realize that Mother Nature is the only artist who could create such a scene.

DIRECTIONS

Beginning at the ranger station on the west slope of the Rincon de la Vieja National Park (see the previous chapter), take the trail uphill toward the volcano. After passing through a large open area, you will go through a small turnstile and into the forest. You will soon come to a trail to your left leading to the Rio Blanco. Ignore this trail and continue uphill to your right. The trail soon splits again; this time, turn left toward Cataratas Escondidas and away from the volcano.

The trail crosses the Rio Blanco approximately 20 minutes from the time you first leave the ranger station. (Caution: this crossing can be tricky during high water.) In about 20 minutes, you will hear the sound of rushing water on your right; if you follow this sound, you will find a hot sulfur stream literally disappearing into a hole in the ground.

Continuing down the main trail, you will cross a large creek (Quebrada Agria) in about 15 minutes. (If you follow this creek upstream for a half mile or so, you will come to a totally private double falls with a nice swimming hole; a little tough to get to, but worth it for those wanting complete privacy.)

A few minutes later, the trail splits again. The left fork leads to Congrejo Falls (see next chapter); the right fork leads to Hidden Falls. As you leave the forest canopy, the trail opens up into a field of tall grass. From here, it's all uphill. The path traverses the hillside and at times brings you back to the fringe of the forest. From here to the ridge about 760 yards above you, the "trail" (a jumble of small boulders strewn along the spine of a steep ridge, some of which have been festooned with arrows pointing the way) enters the realm of arduous. If there is no wind, you will roast; when the vicious volcanic winds howl down from the summit, every step becomes a muscle-wrenching workout. Trust me, you *will* get to the top in about 20 minutes.

Arriving at the ridge crest, you will be facing directly toward a 100-foot waterfall plunging into the canyon below you. Pick your way carefully down the muddy path; shortly you will arrive at the top of a double waterfall, each leg of which looks to be well over 100 feet. DO NOT attempt to scale these falls unless you're a mountain goat.

We bipeds will want to cross the stream *carefully* and head upstream along the right bank to the upper falls and swimming hole, about five minutes away.

CONGREJO FALLS

INTRODUCTION

If Congrejo Fall is one of the jewels of Costa Rica's waterfall system—and it most certainly is—I would have to call it a sapphire. The 80-foot vertical drop alone would be enough to get any tourist's camera clicking, but the *pièce de résistance* of the falls is the impossibly turquoise blue swimming hole below. Never in my life have I encountered such vivid, shimmering blue water.

The water temperature is brisk, but not too cold for a refreshing dip after a hot two-hour hike from the lodge. You can swim across the 40-foot diameter hole to a ledge that allows you to stand completely behind the cascading water. To the left of the falls, a small warm-water thermal spring empties into the pool. All around the swimming hole are a dozen or so giant boulders, many of them almost flat. When I have been there, the dress code seemed to be clothing-optional, at least as long as rangers weren't present. All in all, the perfect recipe for an afternoon of tropical delight.

NOTE: While it would be physically possible to visit Congrejo Falls and Hidden Falls in one day, I would highly recommend that you make a full day out of each waterfall.

DIRECTIONS

For the first leg of the hike, refer to the directions to Hidden Falls in the previous chapter.

From the point that the trail splits, soon after the Quebrada Agria crossing, take the left fork at the edge of the meadow, away from Cataratas Escondidas. (From that point, a ranger estimated the walk to the falls was 45 minutes, which seems about right.)

The trail is easy to follow and well-traveled as it winds through a mix of open meadows and small patches of forest. There is one spot of mud that can be a little messy. Most of the walk is easy to moderate, and you are treated to awesome views of the volcanic peaks on those rare days when the clouds move out of your way.

A half hour from the split with the Cataratas Escondidas trail, you will hear the Rio Congrejo in a canyon to the right of the trail. The trail parallels the rim of the canyon (heading downstream), then plunges rather sharply into the forested gorge. (You may see horses tied up at the top of the drop.)

At the bottom of the steep hill, the trail bends sharply back upstream. From here, it's an easy ten-minute hike along the river-bank up to the falls.

LIBANO FALLS

INTRODUCTION

While not dramatic enough to warrant the label "don't-miss destination," Libano Falls provide an enchanting day trip for those with time to kill in the Lake Arenal community of Tillaran.

Nestled in the forest at the end of an easy ten-minute trail that's fine for kids, this 75-foot cascade feathers out delicately (depending on water levels) across a basalt rock face, to land in a large pool. While not large enough for adults to swim in, it is an excellent children's swimming pool or refreshing bathing pool for grownups.

DIRECTIONS

From the big cemetery on the north side of Tillaran (where the pavement ends), follow the good gravel road toward the village of Libano. The road goes downhill, over a couple of low mountains, and arrives at the river bridge in "downtown" Libano, approximately 5.4 miles from the cemetery.

Cross this bridge. Immediately turn right on the far side of the bridge, swing around to the left, and continue to follow the "main road" for approximately 1 mile. You will reach a small road entering from the right, marked by a sign to Maravilla. Follow this little road about 540 yards, cross a little wooden bridge, and park a few yards uphill on your left.

Follow this trail upstream along the right bank, crossing only once to the left bank. When the stream splits, take the right fork. The easy trail follows the left bank of this creek to the falls, just a few minutes upstream.

Monteverde/San Luis Falls

INTRODUCTION

In my opinion, the Monteverde cloud forest is a bit overrated as a "don't-miss" destination. Although it is unquestionably a beautiful place—and important ecological research is being done there—the hordes of tourists (and resulting gringo prices) are well into the process of killing the *quetzal* that laid the golden egg.

For the crowd-weary nature lover, Monteverde/San Luis Falls offers an excellent opportunity to get away from the bustle, and experience the cloud forest as it used to be before the tourists, and even the cows, appeared on the scene.

But you're going to have to work hard for the opportunity to enjoy this peek into yesteryear. The walk to (and especially back *from*) the falls is nothing short of excruciating. If you're going all the way on foot, plan to leave by 8:00 A.M. if you want to get back by dark. Horses can save a lot of time and aching muscles, but at $8 per hour, you'll pay for that comfort.

Tucked deep into an undisturbed jungle canyon, the waterfall is formed where the river slices through a narrow cleft in the rock, and shoots violently out of the forest to fall approximately 300 feet (with one major break) before landing in a chilly, choppy pool. While a polar bear may enjoy swimming there, I prefer to soak in the falls' awesome beauty from a nearby rock.

The river canyon leading to the falls is almost as dramatic as the cataract itself—but it's no Sunday stroll for young children or out-of-shape adults. Many times you are forced to head up mid-stream, across slippery rocks, boulders, and tree trunks. The final ascent to the falls—full of vicious stinging army ants when I was there—is borderline perilous. Worse than anything in the canyon, however, is the climb back into Monteverde after a full day of hiking. You may want to plan to camp at Miguel Leton's farm at the mouth of the canyon and return to town the next day.

DIRECTIONS

From "downtown" Monteverde, continue on the main road toward the reserve. Pass Hotel Fonda Vela on your right. About 325 feet beyond Hotel Fonda Vela, a small road forks off to your right, which *should* be

marked by a sign pointing to San Luis. Turn right here. In about a half mile, the road forks; stay to your right (downhill). The road soon becomes a horse trail—don't even take a four-wheel drive down this road!—so park before heading downhill.

Walk down a *very* steep rocky horse trail to the bottom of the cliff. The walk, while exhausting, offers fantastic panoramic views all the way across the Nicoya Peninsula; if you look extremely carefully due east, you may be able to spot the falls in the distance.

At the bottom of the cliff, on a small plateau before the road continues downhill again, there is a small aluminum-sided school on your left. Just *before* the building is a wooden gate on your left. Go through the gate and you will be on a horse/jeep trail.

Follow the jeep trail across one good-sized creek, and continue until the trail ends. At the point where the jeep trail peters out to a footpath, there is a wooden gate on your left. Cross through this wooden gate and continue up the footpath leading uphill (toward Miguel Leton's house).

When you arrive at a nice house, the going gets a little tricky. The path seems to disappear, so simply work your way across the pastures behind the house toward the mountains. The river canyon is off to your right. Cross a couple of fences (always close the gates!), then continue downhill to your right toward the river.

Cross the river when you first arrive. There is a rough trail along the right (east) bank of the river for the first half mile or so, but soon you will have to make your way the best you can straight up the middle. In 30 to 45 minutes, you will arrive at two small waterfalls. Between the two falls, a very steep and slippery trail cuts up the right bank. Follow this trail for about five minutes to a dramatic overlook. A rough trail will take you down to the pool at the bottom of the lower falls, but you will need a helicopter to explore the inaccessible upper half of the falls.

NOTE: Remember to leave by 2:00 P.M. if you want to make it back to Monteverde before dark. For a small fee, Miguel Leton will let you pitch a tent on his property if you can't stomach the walk back.

FORTUNA FALLS

INTRODUCTION

After La Paz and Montezuma Falls, Fortuna Falls—a half hour east of Arenal Volcano—probably ranks as one of Costa Rica's most famous (and therefore most popular with tourists) waterfalls. By anyone's description, it is a classic Costa Rican waterfall. Plunging approximately 120 feet in an arching curve out of thick cloud forest, it crashes into a 60-foot pool below. While it is not the most grandiose cataract in the country, it is certainly worth a visit as part of the "Arenal package."

The swimming hole looks inviting, but the water is cold and extremely rough from the falls. The swimming is a little better a few meters downstream. The best swimming hole, however, can be found where the road from the town crosses the river downstream from the falls.

The hour-long steep trek into and out of the canyon may be a little tough for young kids and out-of-shape adults, but it's far from impossible. You can carve a campsite out of the riverbank a few yards downstream from the falls, but bring dry firewood.

DIRECTIONS

One reason Fortuna Falls is so popular with tourists is because popular tourist town of Fortuna, gateway to Arenal Volcano. Buses from San Jose and San Carlos make regular runs to the town, which has plenty of cheap places to eat and sleep.

To find the falls, head west on the road out of town, like you were going to the volcano. One block west of the big central park, turn left at the paved intersection. Cross one bridge. Go about 2 miles and turn right onto a small dirt road that appears to head toward the volcano.

NOTE: If you continue straight on the main road for a half mile or so, you will cross a bridge over the river downstream from the falls; there is an excellent swimming hole with a Tarzan swing here.

To reach the falls, follow the smaller dirt side-road as far as you can (two-wheel drive vehicles are cautioned to park at the base of the steep hill; four-wheel drive vehicles may be able to keep going). Head uphill toward the volcano. You will go up one hill, level out, and go up one more

hill. You will pass a funky little house on your right. Stay left at the fork in the road, heading toward the river canyon.

The trail to the falls turns left off the road about 325 feet past the fork. There is a big grassy camping area beside the road at the trailhead. A few yards off the side of the road is a dramatic overlook taking in the falls and the distant hills. The well-traveled trail to the bottom veers left from the overlook and plunges downhill. The 20-minute descent is extremely steep, so use utmost caution, particularly in muddy conditions.

NOTE: See sections on Rio Tabacon and Arenal Hot Springs.

CHORROS FALLS

INTRODUCTION

One of the most popular falls among the native *ticos* (and, increasingly, tourists) are the twin cataracts, Chorros Falls, near the small town of Tacares. And for good reason: these beautiful falls, 10 miles from Alajuela, are barely an hour's drive from downtown San José; access is via an easy 15-minute walk; a semi–developed campground is moments away; and the falls are fine for families with children.

Best of all, the double falls provide a classic Costa Rican waterfall experience. The first set of falls, barely two minutes from the campground, tumbles over a 120-foot cliff of moss–covered sculpted stone, which breaks the main plume of water into dozens of tiny falls. Another small waterfall enters from the right. The shallow pool below the falls is fair for bathing, but a little rough and a tad cool at 66° F. (18° C.).

The second set of falls, less than 325 feet from the first, has a much different personality. They plunge angrily over the 100-foot cliff in one solid jet of water and crash down into the small pool so violently that swimming is impossible. Vertical cliffs of rock ring the box canyon on three sides. (There's room for a couple of tents here if you want to escape the campground.)

There is one obvious drawback to having such a magnificent natural spectacle so close to a million people. The overload of people (especially on weekends, when Chorros should be avoided) has eroded the riverbank, trampled the vegetation, and—most inexcusable of all—strewn litter all around the falls. On one Monday morning, I found two full-sized bags of garbage tossed into the river just below the falls! While you should not let these distractions keep you from experiencing Chorros, the "purist," will want to seek out some more out-of-the-way falls.

DIRECTIONS

From downtown Alajuela, take the main highway west toward Grecia for approximately 10 miles to the little town of Tacares. Turn right a few meters beyond the church on your right as you enter the town. In one block, bear a *soft* left onto the little road leading uphill. Follow this road approximately 1.7 miles until you reach a cement and chain-link gate on your right. Ignore the "Do Not Enter" signs; if the gate is open, drive through it; if it is locked, park here and walk through it. Whether you walk or drive, head down the hill toward the quarry. Curve around to your left, then immediately fork off to your right onto a wide gravel trail that leads upstream.

(Park here if you drove).

You will probably have to pay a small fee (about $1 per person) before entering the forest.

The trail is easy to follow and is in excellent shape; it even has footbridges so you don't have to get your feet wet. Ten minutes up the trail, after the second footbridge, you will find a campground (crowded on weekends) with picnic tables and fire rings (but no restrooms).

The first falls are 2 minutes upstream from the campground. To reach them from the left bank, cross another bridge over a stream entering from the left. (Your other choice is to cross back over the footbridge and head up the trail along the right bank.)

To reach the second set of falls, walk along the right bank of the small river that enters the main river below the first set of falls (on the same side as the campground). This three-minute walk will take you across the "wall of water," where a dozen or so little waterfalls spring literally from nowhere out of a blank rock face. I have never seen this natural phenomenon anywhere else in Costa Rica.

LA PAZ FALLS

INTRODUCTION

Perhaps the most famous waterfall in all of Costa Rica–and certainly the most accessible–is La Paz Falls. "The Waterfall of Peace" offers visitors of all ages a wonderful opportunity to experience a classic cloud forest cascade without leaving their cars. Reached by an excellent paved road out of Heredia, the waterfall may not offer the most exciting wilderness adventure in Costa Rica, but it does promise a relaxing day trip to the country for city slickers and travelers pressed for time.

The native jungle vegetation around the thundering double cascade is luxuriant, and the ground is literally carpeted with thousands of brilliant impatiens. A lovely pool at the bottom of the falls may look inviting, but the water is warm only to penguins and the rocks are dangerously slick, so I recommend enjoying these falls from a distance.

La Paz Falls is a destination in and of itself, but it is also the gateway to one of the richest waterfall areas in Costa Rica, possibly the world. The next four chapters highlight some of the other wonders that await you just beyond La Paz.

DIRECTIONS

The road to La Paz Falls (and the other waterfalls in the area) begins in downtown Heredia. If you're driving, follow the road uphill into the mountains toward Puerto Viejo (the Puerto Viejo in northeast Costa Rica, not the Puerto Viejo near Cahuita!). You will probably make a couple of wrong turns leaving Heredia, but eventually the roads merge into one main road. Beyond the lovely Colonial village of Barva, the road begins its steep ascent into the hills, passing sugar cane fields, coffee farms, and dairies. The topography and vegetation here are more reminiscent of the San Francisco Bay area than the tropics, and the temperature plummets as you gain altitude and enter the clouds. (It's easy to see why Costa Rica is sometimes compared to Switzerland.)

Approximately 19 miles from Heredia, the road to Puerto Viejo and La Paz Falls forks to the right at Vara Blanca Restaurant and Bar. (Poas Volcano National Park is a few miles farther if you miss the fork to the right.) You will see

a few vestiges of remaining virgin cloud forest as you approach the falls, approximately 5 miles past the restaurant.

Because you cross the bridge over the river only a few meters in front of the falls, it's possible to enjoy the falls from inside your vehicle. However, all but the most hopelessly lazy will want to pull over and walk the 200-foot trail, which begins on the west (left) side of the river. This trail leads visitors beneath a ledge that allows one to stand behind a curtain of water as it plunges over the 60-foot cliff.

The falls in this area are also easily accessible by bus. Take the Puerto Viejo bus from Heredia and ask the driver to drop you off at La Paz Falls (be sure to find out what time the bus heads back to town, however).

SAN FERNANDO FALLS

INTRODUCTION

My nickname for San Fernando Falls—barely a five-minute drive east of its famous kid sister, La Paz Falls— would have to be Deception Falls. Gazing from the cliffside Restaurante Mirador, sipping a cold *cerveza* and munching a plate of hot fried chicken, you may be lulled into thinking that the walk to that beautiful waterfall across the canyon below would be a relaxing way to spend a day in the forest, an hour's stroll at best. Wrong!

The siren song from the rushing water of that postcard-perfect tropical waterfall, seemingly so near, had me seduced in no time. With little more than two hours of daylight left, my friend Karen and I followed the sign indicating the "road" to the waterfall. An hour later, we had slipped, stumbled, and fallen our way to the bottom of a box canyon—and we seemed to be no closer to the falls than when we started. We may as well have been 10,000 miles from fried chicken and beer. Miraculously, we made it out alive before dark.

Karen took the bus (which you can flag down in front of the restaurant) back to San José, but I rested for the night and tackled San Fernando again the next morning. That half-day trip to the falls (which I never reached because you have to swim the final leg) was an unforgettable day in my life, but I can't say I ever want to repeat the experience.

If you are in excellent physical condition, know your way around the woods, have an entire day to kill, and are just a little bit crazy, the trip to San Fernando Falls will not disappoint you. It is an honest-to-Tarzan jungle adventure just a couple of hours from San Jose. If you're in average physical condition, younger than 20 or older than 25, and the least bit sane, enjoy the view from the Restaurante Mirador, and plan to visit one of a half-dozen othe falls in the neighborhood.

Oh, well, if you insist. . .

DIRECTIONS

A couple of miles past (east) La Paz Falls, you'll enter the village of Cinchona. Stop at Restaurante Mirador on your right. The restaurant looks out over the waterfall in the jungle canyon below.

The trail into the canyon begins just past the restaurant. There may or may not be a sign on your right pointing to the cascade. The trail starts off in a coffee farm, which makes it very easy to lose the main path. Generally, head straight downhill until you come to an opening in the natural forest, just to the left of a banana tree (sorry, this is the best I can do for you). Once in the forest, the trail starts out easy to follow, but it's *extremely* steep and slippery, with no switchbacks to soften the grade. There's even a black plastic cable to hold as you head down the steepest parts.

As you approach the bottom of the canyon, the trail becomes increasingly difficult to follow. Just keep aiming downhill toward the sound of rushing water. Eventually, you'll arrive at a beautiful small cataract deep in the canyon. From this point, you will need to battle your way the best you can about a half mile upstream until you arrive at the main falls.

The "trail" upstream is gorgeous, with falls and swimming holes along the river, and a half-dozen other falls entering from your right. It's a jungle adventure of the highest order,

and a trip you'll never forget.

BUT. . .

The trail—both in the canyon and in the river—is extremely dangerous, steep, and slippery. The water is chest-deep in many places, and you literally have to swim the last dozen meters to the main falls. This is a trek for the most die-hard waterfall aficionado only, and not for anyone weak of limb, heart, or courage.

CARIBLANCO FALLS

INTRODUCTION

Quite possibly the most dramatic cascade of all in the "waterfall paradise" east and south of Poas Volcano, Cariblanco Falls is also the least-known. It's certainly the best-hidden, giving it the highest "Tarzan quotient" of all.

Like its nearby cousins Angel/Congo and Toro Amarillo, Cariblanco roars out of deep cloud forest to plunge 500 feet down into a boulder-strewn canyon. Unlike Angel/Congo and Toro Amarillo, however, there is no huge opening in the forest canopy here. The jungle grows in thick and close to the raging water, wrapping the river in a dark green sheath and obliterating the sky. If you want to feel like you just stepped back in time 60 million years, Cariblanco is the ticket to your time machine.

There's only one small catch to enjoying this magical place—to reach the actual falls you must fight your way down one very dangerous river and up another one. The trip requires at least a full-day and you must be a seasoned river-trekker.

Fortunately, for those of us without wings, there is a fairly simple way of enjoying the splendor of Cariblanco Falls without getting our feet wet: via a short trail that leads to a virtually unknown overlook above the mighty falls.

DIRECTIONS

Beginning from Restaurante Mirador in downtown Cinchona, travel east approximately 3 miles, almost to the bottom of the hill, and turn right onto a small gravel road entering at a sharp angle (there will be a sign to some sort of biological reserve). Plunge down into a *steep* canyon for about a half mile, and you will come to an ancient orange bridge that will terrify any intelligent human being; not numbering myself among that elite group, I crossed the bridge in my truck and somehow survived.

Although I made it up to the far side of the canyon in my truck, I would not recommend it to others unless you have four-wheel drive (particularly in the wet season). The rough road snakes uphill, crests at a farm, then plunges down again. The road levels out as it passes through cleared farms. Approximately 1.8 miles from the bridge, before the road plunges down another steep hill, there is a house on your left with a silver metal gate. The house belongs to Marco Miranda; you will need permission from him to cross his farm to the overlook (you'll probably get one of his sons as a guide).

The "trail" begins behind the house and barn, and goes across Señor Miranda's fields, through two gates, before dropping into the forested canyon and the overlook. The walk takes only ten minutes, but you'll probably need a guide to take you there (I suggest a tip of 200 colones). If your appetite is whetted by this spectacle and you can't rest until you get up close and personal with these falls, it can be done—but it won't be easy. Return to the old orange bridge over the Rio Sarapiqui at the bottom of the canyon. Fight your way downstream a mile or so (there is no trail, so it'll be one of the toughest miles of your life),

until the first major stream enters from your right. This is the Rio Cariblanco. Battle your way upstream the best you can until you reach the falls, keeping a sharp eye out for dinosaurs.

NOTE: This route is arduous, to say the least, and life-threatening to say the most. Only those people with a lot of experience hiking in whitewater should even think about attempting it. I would suggest you camp at the bridge the night before to give yourself a full day to reach the falls and return, and pack extremely lightly for the trip. There's no need for me to attempt detailed directions to the falls because you'd drop this book in the water; if you know enough to make this trip, you can follow your own instincts. While I don't recommend this trip to most people, those who do make the journey will have a day in the jungle—the real jungle—that they will never forget. I promise.

ANGEL/CONGO FALLS

INTRODUCTION

Of the 30 or so waterfalls in this book, none are more deserving of the clichéd adjectives "breathtaking" and "awe-inspiring" than Rio Angel Falls (also known locally as Congo Falls). Despite its name, this raging torrent of hydro-energy is no angel—it's 300 feet of pure devil. Considering the fact that this spectacular water show is a fairly easy 35-minute jaunt from a highway (with a public bus), Angel Falls, in my opinion, ranks as one of the "don't miss" waterfall experiences in Costa Rica.

Don't expect a warm, lazy tropical experience at Cascada Congo (named after the ever-present troop of howler monkeys that hang out around the falls). The sheer energy of the churning water creates a ceaseless, blustery, wet wind that will chill you right through a rain parka; it has made tree growth around the pool impossible, creating a huge crack in the cloud forest canopy. Swimming in the pool itself would be foolhardy at best, but there's an excellent blue swimming hole (with diving rock) about 325 feet downstream.

Angel Falls is remarkably easy to get to, and—except for one fairly tricky stream crossing at the beginning—should be fine for children and those in less-than-perfect physical condition. Enjoy this waterfall now; in a few years, I predict it will be just one more crowded tourist attraction.

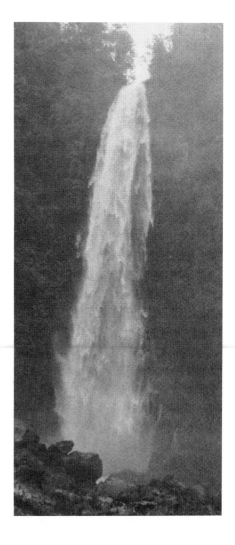

DIRECTIONS

Beginning at Restaurante Mirador in downtown Cinchona, follow the main road eastward down a steep continuous hill for 3.2 miles. Although there probably is no sign, the stream at the bottom of the hill is the Rio Angel. If you get to a toll booth, you have gone too far; turn around and go back to the first bridge.

The trail begins as a small jeep trail on the east (toll booth) side of the river. Four-wheel drive vehicles may be able to go a short way up this trail; park other cars on the shoulder. The jeep trail follows the right bank upstream for a short distance. It is possible to camp along this track, but the ground is soggy. In about 325 feet, the road peters out into a footpath that soon crosses the river. There are a couple of options at the crossing; any of them are a bit tricky, so be careful in the swift water.

From the left (west) bank, the trail initially cuts up a small steep hill, but becomes remarkably level and easy as you follow the ridge of the canyon along the left riverbank for a half mile or so. The trail takes a dip to the right back toward the river, but soon levels out again. You will pass one nice cascade hidden by trees, and reached by a very rough, steep "path."

A little farther along, you will pass one of the best diving cliffs in Costa Rica, extending approximately 30 feet down into a crystal-clear, *cold* swimming hole.

The waterfall itself appears in another 500 feet or so. Possibly the most spectacular cascade within easy reach in all of Costa Rica, Congo Falls plummets 300 feet or so straight down into an open jungle clearing.

Don't even think about swimming here. The water is extremely rough—and cold—and the wind whipping off the falls blows continuously, making it "rain" on even rare sunny days. Save swimming for the diving hole downstream.

Rio Toro Amarillo Falls

INTRODUCTION

The Yellow Bull River, which rampages out of the east flank of Poas Volcano on its mad dash toward the Caribbean Sea, certainly reminds one of a charging bull, but what I've seen of the water is all white.

I've never managed to schedule the time and have the energy it would take to fully explore the gorge below the huge main falls (I understand it is full of other smaller falls), but the granddaddy waterfall at the tip of the canyon certainly calls to the wild savage in me. Some day I'll explore it if the power companies don't beat me to it.

The full-sized river blasts out of deep cloud forests and plummets in a frenzied torrent to the huge red-rock bowl approximately 300 feet below. The churning water races along through other smaller rock-lined pools and disappears into a steep-walled jungle canyon, challenging the river rat to follow. Unfortunately, the almost-vertical cliffs around the falls prevent one from approaching the river from that direction, and the hike upstream (if possible) would require at least an overnight expedition from the highway bridge downstream.

My biggest fear as I write this (in 1993) is that the gorge–and possibly the main falls–will soon be destroyed by a massive hydroelectric project. My limited Spanish prevented me from getting the full details from the construction crews, and I later heard mixed reports of what was going on at Toro Amarillo. A sick feeling in my gut tells me that this treasure will soon be flooded in the name of greed.

DIRECTIONS

For people with private vehicles (the nearest bus stop, on the highway connecting Puerto Viejo to San Carlos, is 10 miles away), a trip to the top of the falls via a good dirt road is a must. From La Paz Falls, continue on the highway toward Puerto Viejo, passing San Fernando, Cariblanco, and Angel/Congo Falls.

Approximately 8 miles past La Paz, soon after you pass through a small toll booth, the road will divide. At this intersection, turn left away from Puerto Viejo toward Ciudad Quesada (commonly known as San Carlos); this is where you would change buses, also. In about

another mile, a paved road will turn off to your left. Look carefully for a yellow sign pointing to a hydroelectric project.

Along the 9.5-mile road to the trailhead, you will pass through a lot of depressing hydroelectric construction. After passing the main construction site, keep your eye out for these landmarks in the next 5 miles: a building on your left, a bridge over a blue-water creek, and another huge building on your right. Approximately 325 feet past this building, you will see a sign (really!) to the falls.

Park here on the side of the road. (If you were to continue along this road, you would ultimately arrive in the tourist town of Sarchi in about an hour. This little-known pass across the north side of Poas offers stunning mountain scenery and dramatic views of the central valley—I highly recommend this alternate route.)

A very well-developed and easy trail leads from the right side of the road to an overlook about 100 yards away. The flat grassy area at the overlook is about the only place to camp, but it's rather exposed to wind and rain.

An extremely steep and slippery trail leads off to your right approximately 650 feet to another overlook offering a more dramatic view of the falls across the canyon. Unfortunately, this is as close as most of us will ever get to this jungle jewel.

LAGUNA KOPPER

INTRODUCTION

While neither a waterfall nor a hot spring, Laguna Kopper has been included in this book because it makes an ideal base camp for those wanting to explore the waterfall-rich area east and south of Poas Volcano.

Although Laguna Kopper is within a half-hour's drive of at least seven major waterfalls, its much lower elevation places it in an entirely different ecosystem—much more akin to the balmy, muggy Caribbean coast than the chilly, windy cloud forests that spawn the falls.

Barely a ripple disturbs the surface of this little lake, and the jungle vegetation ringing the shore is reflected as if in a mirror. The water is clear and almost bathtub-warm. After so many chilly mountain streams, this is the perfect place to kick back after a hard day of trekking.

There is a large, level grassy area for camping right by the lakeshore, and there's even a small boat ramp. Best of all, it's free—and the only gringo you're going to see will be someone who bought this book.

The only minor drawback to Laguna Kopper is that you need a four-wheel drive vehicle (except in the driest times) to negotiate the last 975 feet or so to the lakeshore—trust me, I speak from hard-learned experience! The two dirt roads leading from the highway (and public transportation) 1.7 miles away, have some bad spots as well, although I was able to negotiate them successfully in my two-wheel drive truck in the dry season.

DIRECTIONS

From the toll booth east of Angel/Congo Falls, continue east toward Puerto Viejo. Where the road forks, turn left, away from Puerto Viejo, as if you were heading to Rio Toro Amarillo Falls. You will pass through the little village of Rio Cuatro, then cross the bridge over the Rio Cuatro.

About .35 miles past the bridge, a small dirt road turns off to the right. Turn right here, then bear around to the left, where the road passes between a big warehouse on your left and a little cemetery on your right. (Caution: there are some tough mud spots here.)

Approximately 1 mile from the highway, a smaller dirt road

comes in from the right. You will probably be able to see the lake down and to your right. Follow this little road (which hugs a ridge above the north shore of the lake) for about a half mile. Ignore all the "Private Property" signs, and turn right into the rutted, muddy jeep trail to your right. Park here if you don't have four-wheel drive.

The lake and campground are at the end of this little road, about 975 feet farther.

Braulio—Carillo National Park

INTRODUCTION

Barely a half-hour's drive east from the madness of downtown San José, the sprawling and rugged Braulio-Carillo National Park is, without a doubt, home to many waterfalls. I'd love to explore this cloud forest and send you back reports of waterfall treasures untold.

Unfortunately, all is not calm beneath the serene veneer of the verdant cloud forest canopy. A well-armed band of *banditos* has entrenched itself in the park, ready to pounce, jaguar-like, on unsuspecting tourists as they explore the trails winding through the park. To my knowledge, no tourists have been shot—yet—but several have been tied up, and reports of thefts of cars, cameras, money, and passports continue to pile up.

This is disappointing, to put it mildly, and I certainly hope armed attacks against tourists don't become common in other parts of Costa Rica, as they have in many Central American countries.

So far, I have never been robbed while exploring any of the waterfalls in this book, and my car has always been intact when I returned. However, I have been robbed more than a dozen times in my ten months in Costa Rica, including very serious car burglaries in which I lost virtually everything.

A few tips:

➤ Stay out of Braulio-Carillo National Park, downtown San José, Limon, and Puntarenas. Period.

➤ Try to camp in developed campsites with other people.

➤ If camping in isolated areas, break down camp every morning, and stash your stuff deep in the brush before taking even short day hikes.

➤ If you must leave your car unattended overnight, park it at a *tico's* house in the area, lock it securely, and carry all money and important papers with you.

TURRIALBA FALLS

INTRODUCTION

This series of three small falls, only minutes from the town of Turrialba, provides an easily accessible glimpse of what the forests southeast of San José once looked like before the slash-and-burners invaded. A five-minute drive from the old Limon Highway and an easy five-minute walk brings you to the lower falls. This 40- to 50-foot vertical drop lands in a small, rough pool. Bright impatiens carpet the rocks around the tumbling water, making an excellent picnic site that's fine for little children. There is room for one or two small tents, as well.

Upstream are two more sets of smaller cascades, each about 20 feet high. The "trail," which begins along the right flank of the main falls, diminishes to mid-stream wading, It is a bit trickier to negotiate than the lower falls—particularly for small kids—but the bathing pools are far superior. These falls are popular with the locals, so keep your swimsuit on.

DIRECTIONS

Using a compass and sextant and the Southern Cross as your guides (there are no road signs), negotiate your way through the center of the town of Turrialba, and find your way to the road to Siquirres. (You might want to pick up some food and drinks for a picnic at the falls.)

Toward the edge of town, on your right, locate the Panaderia of the Americas. Turn right here. Follow this road around the curve to the right. Continue to the stop sign, turn left, then immediately bear to your right (following the signs to the "Taller Publico Turrialba").

Bear left onto the dirt road toward the "Taller Publico." The falls are a half mile down this dirt road. You'll pass some ponds and the *taller* (mechanic) on your left and an industrial building on your right. Continue to the first little concrete bridge over a nondescript stream. Cross the bridge and park on the right in front of a little metal gate.

The trail begins at the gate. Head upstream along the left bank. The trail is easy and well-marked as it heads into the jungle along the left bank of a rushing

mountain stream. The trail ends in about five minutes, and you must complete the last 165 feet or so in the stream or along the right bank.

A steep and slippery path leads up the right flank of the falls to a second set of cataracts with a better swimming hole and a water temperature of 66° F. (17° C.). For the best swimming hole, however, you'll need to battle your way upstream for another 650 feet or so.

HITOY-CERERE FALLS

INTRODUCTION

The mighty Talamanca Mountains, which crumple and drain the entire southeast quarter of Costa Rica, cover one of the greatest wilderness areas left in Central America—and they are without a doubt a tropical waterfall lover's Nirvana.

Gazing at all those squiggly little brown and blue lines on Talamanca topo maps never fails to bring out the Joseph Conrad in me. Unfortunately (fortunately?), red lines—indicating roads—are practically non-existent on the maps.

It would take weeks of arduous backpacking to scratch the surface of the hundreds of steep, remote jungle canyons (every one with a stream), but I can only imagine the magical rewards for one's efforts. Fortunately for most of us, there is one fairly easy way to peer into the mysterious world of the Talamancas: Hitoy-Cerere Biological Reserve.

Virtually unknown to the throngs of tourists who drive by it every day on their way to Cahuita and Puerto Viejo, Hitoy-Cerere looms in cloud-shrouded majesty behind the endless expanse of banana plantations that have poisoned the earth and the people south of Limon.

Trying to find the place by car is an adventure right out of Conrad's own imagination (not one single sign, but the roads are excellent, amazingly enough).

But all your cussing and sweating will instantly be forgotten the moment you come around a bend in the river and behold a sight that few gringos have seen before: a creek erupting seemingly from nowhere out of the thick vegetation along the steep right bank, and tumbling approximately 120 feet into a tiny pool in the rocks. A small falls drains that pool into the warm jade-green waters of the Cerere River, and the two streams merge into a cauldron of whitewater. The most remarkable "boulders" (composed of thousands of small river stones cemented together by some unbelievably powerful natural force) lay scattered about, offering superb picnicking and diving opportunities in and around the river's the swimming hole

It's truly a magical spot, one you won't want to leave. If you want to spend the night, there is a lovely—but technically illegal—campsite about 250 feet downstream.

If you have the time and energy, I would highly recommend checking out another set of falls about a half-hour's slog upstream. These falls, while not quite so impressive at 80 to 90 feet, are tucked away in the jungle about 500 feet up a small creek that enters the river from the left. You're literally swallowed up by the rain forest in your own little Garden of Eden. There's no more perfect place to steal away with your lover for a little Gringo Tarzan and Jane fantasy.

DIRECTIONS

Head south along the Atlantic Highway from Limon toward Cahuita. Approximately 23 miles south of Limon, cross a huge bridge over the Rio Estrella. Drive through banana plantations for about a mile to your first right turn. (I believe this is as close as public buses can get you.) Turn right here.

From here, you're on your own. It would take an entire book to attempt to give directions to the park, even if I were able to. This would be an excellent place to practice your Spanish; if you're able to make this trip, you're all set to find your way from San Diego to Tierra del Fuego with no problem.

To start you out: turn right onto the gravel road from the main highway. Drive several miles until you see a large wooden bridge on your right. Cross this bridge—you heard me, cross it! On the other side, turn left. Good luck from this point. Oh yeah, be careful of trains that share trestles with cars driving in the other direction. . .

If it's any help to you, here are the directions I received from a man at the first bridge, verbatim: "Pass airport. Pass Finca 6. Pass Finca 5. Cross bridge (the one you share with the train) to Finca 12. Go to Finca 16. Pass Fincas 15 and 14. Go through Cara-gena. Go into the mountains and into the park."

One warning: the road to the park is very good, fine for two-wheel drive cars—until the last half mile! If by some miracle you find your way through the bananas and into the hills, you'll arrive at a nice two-story house in the middle of nowhere on your right. Bear left here, uphill.

In approximately a half mile, you'll come to a corral on your left. Park your two-wheel drive car here and walk the final half mile to the ranger station (four-wheel vehicles should be okay all the way to the park headquarters).

From the ranger station (where you will be charged a small fee), turn right toward the river. Cross the river, and begin working your way upstream the best you can. It's easiest to cross the "island" of vegetation on the far side of the river and walk along the dry river bed.

Cross the river again and continue up the rocks along the left bank. Follow the rocks for 325 to 650 feet. Straight ahead, across a narrow little channel of river, the trail heads straight into the jungle about 230 feet parallel to the left bank of the main river channel. The trail can get tricky; you're actually walking in a swampy little creek much of the time.

In a few minutes, the trail reappears at the river. Cross here and continue up the rocks along the right bank. Just keep crossing and recrossing the river the best you can, working to stay on the rocks as you head upstream. The jungle soon closes in on the river, and as soon as you enter this remarkable canyon, all problems are forgotten.

The falls appear out of nowhere along the right bank about ten minutes into this canyon. There is an excellent swimming hole here in the river with a water temperature of 72° F. (24° C.), and a huge flat rock perfect for picnicking and sun-bathing. The other, smaller falls await you about 30 minutes upstream. A small rough trail of sorts begins along the left river-bank, but doesn't last for long. Work your way up the river, which soon breaks out of the steep canyon and opens up again.

Approximately a half mile upstream, a small creek enters from the left bank. It's very easy to miss, being partially hidden by tall grass and acacia trees. Follow this little creek upstream about 325 feet, take the left bank over some big rocks, and you'll arrive at yet another beautiful waterfall.

SALTO AND PALMITOS FALLS

INTRODUCTION

Little-known Tapanti National Park, an hour's drive southeast of Cartago, is a dream come true for lovers of small, "intimate" waterfalls. As you make your way up any of the creeks that branch off from the Rio Orosi Canyon, you expect to spy hobbits and leprechauns ducking behind trees. The mighty Rio Orosi forms the heart and soul of Tapanti. A half-dozen shredded yellow rubber rafts in the gorge bear mute testimony to the power in those frothing waters. Still, it's amazingly easy to enjoy an unforgettable day hike into the canyon, at least in the dry season. You can explore a dozen or more small cascades in one day, but two falls—Salto and Palmitos—are the crown jewels of the canyon.

Salto Falls are those you see in the picture whenever Tapanti is written up in a guidebook or tourist publication. From a distance, they appear to spring from a hole in the mountainside, crash and tumble over a sheer rock wall some 300 feet high, and then disappear again into the belly of the forest. Ninety percent of those who see Salto Falls do so from the overlook at the "mirador," a couple of miles from the park entrance. It is a pretty view, but the true explorer will want to get up close and personal.

Unfortunately, that's easier said than done. The path upstream over a half-dozen lower falls has been conquered by precious few—and I must admit I'm not a member of that exclusive club. I somehow managed to scramble up three of the lower falls, and I could see and hear the main falls some 975 feet upstream, but falls number four were my "Waterfall Waterloo." It would take ropes and pulleys to reach the top—so I headed for easier quarry: Palmitos Falls, an hour's walk up the river gorge.

While not spectacular in and of themselves, Palmitos Falls rate high on my list because they lie deep in the Orosi River Gorge. As you continue your hike upstream from Salto Creek, the canyon walls get steeper, and the river gets narrower and swifter. Creeks have only one way to enter the river now: straight down. A half-dozen falls plummet into the gorge in less than a mile.

As the jungle-covered rock walls close in (making trekking a bit tricky, but not impossible), the

"queen waterfall" of the canyon—Palmitos—gushes out of the left bank to drop 50 feet directly into the river. Just beyond is yet another waterfall and a chilly swimming hole, then the gorge is entirely sealed by a jumble of massive boulders. Sitting on one of the picnic boulders nearby, enjoying the haunting scenery (most often cloaked in brooding clouds), you half expect to see a dinosaur stick its head out from behind a boulder.

If someone in your group wants a more relaxed way to enjoy the splendors of Tapanti, check out Sendero Oropendula (Bellbird Trail) just inside the park gates on your right. An excellent all-weather trail leads to a lovely swimming hole with diving rocks, as well as several picnic shelters with tables and grills. It's a great place for the kids, the softer-of-body, and the plain exhausted.

No camping is allowed in the park (ridiculous, considering the set-up at Oropendula!), but there is a primitive "campsite" at the Orosi River Bridge a couple of miles before you get to the park gates.

For dinner, check out the fresh trout (*trucha*) at Restaurante Rio Macho, a few miles farther down the road toward Cartago at the next bridge.

DIRECTIONS

NOTE: These directions are entirely from memory, as the notepad they were written on was destroyed in a wreck. I *believe* they are accurate.

To reach Tapanti National Park, take the road southeast out of Cartago toward Paraiso, then continue to follow the signs to Orosi. The public bus runs regularly at least as far as Orosi (where there are two nice developed hot springs to be discussed later in the book).

Continue through town and keep on the main road all the way until it ends at the park. It begins to get a little rough beyond Orosi, but passenger cars are fine. There is a rough campground at the big metal bridge a couple of miles before the park.

The park is open daily from 8:00 A.M. to 4:00 P.M. (no overnight camping), and there is a small entrance fee. Once inside the park, the road is excellent and points of interest are well-marked. Approximately 1 mile beyond the park gates, the trailhead for the Sendero Oropendula is on your right. In another 1.5 miles or so, there is a beautiful view of the canyon. Approximately 2.1 miles into the park, you will see a sign to Sendero La Pava on your right. This is the trailhead to the falls.

(For a beautiful view of Salto Falls, follow the road just beyond the Sendero La Pava trailhead, and walk up the short trail behind the picnic tables on your left. If you continue up this road for another 12 miles or so, you will arrive at a beautiful 75-foot cascade with an icy swimming hole right beside the road—an excellent Tapanti waterfall alternative for those not wishing to hike into the Orosi gorge.)

To reach both Salto and

Palmitos Falls, park at the Sendero La Pava trailhead. The trail leads downhill to the river via an easy ten-minute walk with switchbacks. (Caution: place some sort of marker where the trail opens onto the gravel bar alongside the river so you can recognize it on your return trip.)

Once in the gorge, head upstream the best you can. There is no real trail, but the walk is quite easy at first. Try to begin your walk along the right bank of the river so you do not miss Quebrada Salto (Salt Creek) coming in from the right.

The best way I can think to describe this spot is where a good-sized stream enters from the right in a small waterfall that spills into the main river among some *huge* boulders that look like they would make a good run in a whitewater kayak (that's the best I can do. . .).

To reach Salto Falls—make that *attempt* to reach—battle your way upstream the best you can. The falls get increasingly rough to negotiate. I went along the right bank for the first two falls, then groped along on my belly on an extremely steep and slippery trail along the left bank of the third falls. I finally called it quits at the fourth set of falls, although I could see signs that some real idiots had continued to the huge falls about 975 feet up-stream. I am not recommending you follow in their muddy footprints.

Instead, I recommend heading back to the main river gorge and continuing upstream another hour or so to Palmitos Falls. As you get deeper into the gorge and the walls steepen, the going gets a little trickier. You'll pass a half-dozen pretty falls formed by streams entering the canyon on both sides.

The scenery is nothing short of enchanting by the time you spy Palmitos Falls pouring in from the left. Naturally, the last few yards are extremely rough going, but the huge picnic rocks and swimming hole in this magic spot will make your huffing and puffing worth it.

SAVEGRE/SAN GERARDO FALLS

INTRODUCTION

Hidden away deep in the mountains between Cartago and San Isidro, the tiny dairy village of San Gerardo is a sort of undiscovered Monteverde. (If you want to see what Monteverde was like before the tourist invasion, this is your chance.) The scenery (and nighttime temperatures!) here are more reminiscent of the Alps than the steamy tropics, but the waterfall in the Savegre River is classic Costa Rican.

About an hour's walk from the ritzy Albergue de Montaña Savegre lodge, the chilly waters of the Savegre have gouged out the sheer granite walls. The cascade pours out of the narrow crevice, freefalls for 80 to 90 feet, and then fans out over the rock walls before landing in a deep pool (a little rough and cold for swimming).

A visit to these falls would make an idyllic way to spend half a day, or you can camp overnight at one of the many nice streamside campsites—including a midstream gravel bar below the falls.

DIRECTIONS

From San José, take the Pan-American Highway south, travel through Cartago, and head up into the mountains to kilometer post 80. Just past K–80, there will be a sign indicating an *escuela* (school). Turn right here onto a small dirt road toward the village of San Gerardo (there may be a small sign). This excellent little road plunges into a canyon and passes through lush dairy lands as it parallels the headwaters of the Rio Savegre.

In about 6 miles, the road arrives at Albergue de Montaña Savegre, a very nice-looking (and expensive?) lodge.

The road continues to parallel the river for about 540 yards or so. When the main road veers off to the right away from the river, there is a grassy parking area beside the river on your left. A wide trail begins at the gate here. Do not block the gate with your car.

Cross the bridge over the river. This little dirt road splits about 120 feet beyond the bridge. Turn right onto the smaller dirt road (heading downstream along the left bank). The road comes out into a clearing on your right.

Bear right here onto the footpath through the pasture, past the "NO" sign.

The trail is very moderate and easy to follow for a half mile or so, and there are several excellent campsites along the way. This nice little trail ends at a pretty—but freezing—swimming hole with two gravesites beside it. This is the end of the easy walk.

Cross the river here. What should be an easy crossing is made tough by a giant boulder on the far (right) bank. You must aim your crossing to land on the left (downstream) side of the boulder. The trail continues downstream through forest along the right bank. It passes a small waterfall in the river, then skirts the top of a steep ravine. Careful!

At the bottom of the ravine is a magical spot with a small waterfall, a cave, giant boulders, a swimming hole, etc. It's definitely worth a side trip, and there's even room on a huge flat rock to place a small self-standing tent.

The trail vacillates between tough and easy for the next 760 yards or so. Soon after the trail squeezes between two boulders, it arrives at the river again. Cross here to the left bank and continue downstream. The last 650 feet or so are *extremely* steep as the trail traverses the falls from the top to the bottom. The last 120 feet of the "trail" is in a small side stream that makes a nice little waterfall itself.

DIAMANTE FALLS

INTRODUCTION

Diamante Falls, while in a relatively low mountain range, has one vertical drop of 450 feet and several smaller falls above, making it one of the highest waterfalls in Costa Rica. (In all my travels, I've never discovered conclusively where *the* tallest falls in Costa Rica are.)

During the rainy season, Diamante is one dramatic sight to behold. The high water can make it one dangerous sight to behold, as well. Unfortunately, after about mid-January, the water level drops precipitously, and much of the impact is lost.

To truly experience the wonders of Diamante, one needs to explore the remote upper falls and spend a night in the "rock castle" there. However, that adventure requires ropes and climbing equipment—not to mention the expensive services of a trained guide—so Yours Truly can't give you a firsthand report.

If you have an extra day to kill, Diamante is certainly worth the two-hour round-trip hike. However, if your time is limited, enjoy the view of the falls from a distance, and continue down the road a piece to her fairer kid sister, Santo Cristo Falls.

DIRECTIONS

From the city of San Isidro General, take the highway west toward Dominical. (Obviously, if you're beginning in Dominical, take the road toward San Isidro.) High in the mountains approximately 10 miles west of San Isidro, you will arrive in the little mountain village of Tinamaste. You will pass a hotel/bar, then a small store, both on your left.

Just before the little store on your left (Pulperia Las Brisas), across the street from a small government building, a gravel road will enter from your left. This is the road to Diamante Falls.

The road will descend rather rapidly into a canyon. You will cross one bridge, and go through the tiny village of Las Tumbas, where you will cross a second bridge. Approximately 2.5 miles from where you left the highway, just beyond the second bridge, there will be a little brown house on your left (it was for sale in 1993). You may be charged a small entrance fee if anyone is home; the trail itself begins behind the house. Cross the little creek behind the house, then bear right over the little rock-filled pasture. Cross another little creek, then enter the woods.

The trail is well-marked and easy to follow at this point. You'll cross one gate and continue straight; then you will cross another gate and continue straight again. Bear left uphill past the second gate; the waterfall will come into view on a cliff ahead and to your left.

At this point, the trail becomes easy to lose in the tall grass among all the cow trails. Go through another gate and work your way uphill the best you can. Eventually, toward the back right corner of the pasture, there's a ravine on your left with a huge dead log. I followed this ravine to the river, though there was no real trail.

Pick your way the best you can along the left bank or up the middle of the river. Occasionally,

you'll make out vague vestiges of a trail.

When you come to a small waterfall with a pool, cross to the other bank and finish up on the right side. Naturally, the last 200 feet are the toughest, with some big slippery rocks to conquer, but you'll get there.

A horrendously steep trail (local guides use ropes) heads up the left side of the main falls toward a string of 25- to 75-foot falls, which I understand are quite beautiful. DO NOT attempt this trail without a guide, and plan to spend at least a full day—better yet, stay overnight, if you plan to do this trip.

The "trail" back to the road—or what there is of it—is easier to follow downstream if you very carefully keep your eye out for faint machete marks left by local guides. Miraculously, I reappeared in the pasture at the same point where I left it.

NAUYACA/SANTO CRISTO FALLS

INTRODUCTION

You can't ask a doting mother to choose her "favorite" child, and you can't ask the author of a book on Costa Rican waterfalls to choose his "favorite" waterfall. They *all* have something special to offer, or they wouldn't be in this book.

But if you were to ask me which waterfall in this book provides the quintessential tropical waterfall experience with the least amount of hassle (the most waterfall bang for the buck, as it were), I would have to answer Nauyaca (a.k.a San Cristobal or Santo Cristo).

Santo Cristo offers everything a winter-weary gringo could hope for in a waterfall and then some—awesome beauty, warm water, a superb swimming hole, and fairly easy access. I challenge you to visit Santo Cristo Falls and not have a good time.

I must admit I was a tad dubious of the glowing praise I'd heard about Santo Cristo on my first visit. The logged-over ranchland flanking the river, while pretty, wasn't quite National Geographic material. My mood brightened considerably when the double falls, 140-foot upper falls

and 75-foot lower falls, came into view; I became a Santo Cristo junkie the moment I dove into her warm-water pool.

While only a few yards of river separate the two cascades, they are amazingly different in appearance and personality. The upper falls pour over a 140-foot sheer cliff of rock that appears as so many giant stone obelisks. The water crashes on to giant rocks below and there is little space for swimming. There is, however, space for one or two small, self-supporting tents on the shelf of flat rock.

Seconds later, the river fans out into a much more delicate and gentle pattern as it tumbles over a 75-foot rock face as wide as it is tall. Below this beautiful backdrop—but still in plain view of the raging upper falls—is one of the best swimming holes in all of Costa Rica: approximately 50 to 70 feet across, deeper than I can dive, and—best of all—78° F. (25.5° C.).

The trail alongside the river is in excellent shape with steps and handrails, and there are inner tubes available for floating. The owner of the land alongside the falls, Lulo, was planning to build a small snack bar and picnic ground. We were charged a $5 admission fee on a Saturday, but there was not another soul around the two times I visited during the week.

Depending on how far you take your car (four-wheel drive can get within a mile; regular cars or public bus within a couple of miles), the falls should be accessible to most anyone, and the trail from the road is easy and safe. Go for the day, or do yourself a favor and spend the night.

DIRECTIONS

There are three ways to reach Santo Cristo: on foot overland, wading up stream, or on horseback. For any of these options, you need to go to the town of Platanillo in the mountains on the road between San Isidro de General and Playa Dominical.

From San Isidro, drive west (check public bus schedules in town) toward Dominical for about 14.5 miles. You'll see a large tourist restaurant and bar on your right in the village of Platanillo. Approximately 1.6 miles (beyond this tourist stop, a small dirt road enters from the left, marked by a sign reading:

"Entrance to Libano/Cataratas Nauyaca 3 km." (Driving from Dominical, this will be a right turn 5.8 miles from the coast road.)

Park here if you do not have four-wheel drive; the road should be okay otherwise. The road plunges down a fairly steep canyon (a *hot* walk back) to arrive at the river in about 1.2 miles. There is an excellent campsite at the end of this road on the beach below the swinging pedestrian bridge. The quickest way to the falls (approximately an hour) is walking overland, but it can be hot, and you *will* be charged a land-crossing fee of about $5 per person per day; double that if you plan to spend the night.

From where you park along the river, head upstream on the left bank via a well-defined horse trail. In a few minutes, the horse trail will cross the river and head uphill, swinging away from the right bank. In about 20 minutes, you will pass a nice small house on your right, the home of Lulo Jiminez. (Pay your entrance fee here, or Lulo will collect it later at the falls.)

Twenty minutes or so beyond Lulo's house, you will pass a weather-beaten derelict shed on

your left. The trail to the falls will be on your left 40 yards beyond this building, just past two black boulders also on your left. Look *very carefully* for a small gate at the point where two barbed-wire fences join.

Once you've located the gate, the trail itself is well-marked and easy to follow (with a few muddy spots) as it winds its way for 540 yards to the falls. You will pass a small wooden dressing room, beyond which the trail divides: left takes you to the lower falls and swimming hole; right to the dramatic upper falls.

If you have more time (about two hours each way) and want to avoid the hot sun and the land-crossing fee, I would highly recommend hiking the river itself — at least during the dry season. When you first start out from the parking area, you will actually be in a channel forming the left side of an island; this is no problem, but remember to stay to your right on the return trip.

There are a few tricky spots along the way, but for the most part it's 60 to 90 minutes of rock-hopping. If you don't break your leg on one of the hundreds of slippery rocks, you will come

to a fork in the river. If you're planning to spend the night, there's a nice campsite on a small beach on the right side.

To reach the falls, bear to your right, and keep to the right bank. You begin a gentle climb as the river enters a narrow canyon with a dozen or so small falls, both in the river channel itself and in several smaller side streams. The path is amazingly easy to follow along the right bank, and there's a beautiful swimming hole every five minutes, so take your time and enjoy yourself. You will be steered into crossing to the left bank before reaching the main falls.

The other option is the luxury route, via horseback. For about $35 per person (more for overnight stays), Lulo will meet you at the highway in Platanillo, lead you to the falls, feed you lunch, and have you back before dark—and you never have to lift a finger, a foot, or a heavy pack. Call for reservations a couple of days ahead at 71-09-44. If you need the services of an English-speaking guide, ask around for Woody at the Bellavista Lodge in Dominical.

DOMINICALITO FALLS

INTRODUCTION

At no more than 50 feet, these pretty little falls are hardly Costa Rica's most awe-inspiring cataract. But I include them here because they are just minutes from Dominical, they are a three-minute stroll from the road, and they are just down the road from guides to Santo Cristo Falls.

With a safe and warm swimming hole (complete with Tarzan swing) and such easy access, Dominicalito is a perfect place for the kids and an excellent place to take a mid-day break from the heat at the beach.

DIRECTIONS

Drive south on the main beach road past Dominical, approximately 2.5 miles past the river bridge. On your right, look for a sign saying "Cafeteria." On your left, look for a sign saying "Bella Vista Guest Lodge." Turn left toward the lodge. Immediately bear right, still following signs toward Bella Vista. A fairly rough road crosses a creek.

Beyond the creek, park at the next Bella Vista sign. Directly across the road from the sign, you'll hear the falls in a little grotto on your right.

The trail begins behind an old barbed-wire fence on the right side of the road. The falls and swimming hole are at the end of an easy 325-foot trail.

RIO CATARATA FALLS

INTRODUCTION

A few miles below pineapple-rich Buenos Aires, the Pan-American Highway begins its 35-mile journey through the "Valle de General"—an odd name, because the river on your left is known as the Rio Terraba at this point.

Along the right (west) side of the highway is a low but steep ridge of mountains, drained every couple of miles by small side rivers that empty into the main river.

I believe that every one of these streams has a waterfall of some stature at some point, and eventually I hope to explore them all. The three I have explored—Rio Catarata, Rio Puerto Nuevo, and Rio Palma Norte—have all rewarded me with nice falls only a few minutes' walk upstream from the highway. All three of these small falls could be enjoyed in less than a day.

A few miles south of the big river bridge in Brujos, the aptly-named Rio Catarata is an excellent gateway to the waterfall-rich Valle de General. The "river" (actually two streams) offers travel-weary tourists a chance to visit two nice falls within ten minutes of the highway.

Barely out of sight of the highway bridge (clearly marked with a sign indicating the Rio Catarata), the main (left) fork of the stream drops and feathers out over a vertical rock wall approximately 200 feet high. The water is warm enough for a refreshing shower, but there is no swimming pool. The water level at this waterfall, as with others in the area, drops sharply after mid-January.

Ten minutes up the smaller (right) fork is another cascade with a completely different look and personality. Here, time and water have carved a huge granite bowl out of the forest, and the cliffs above you are more than 90 degrees; you are literally swallowed up by the jungle. At the rear of this cleft in the rain forest, a 35-foot plume of water pours into a small pool that is excellent for bathing, but not large enough for swimming.

DIRECTIONS

Approximately 9 miles south of Buenos Aires on the Pan-American Highway, cross the bridge over the Rio General at the village of Brujos, and continue south toward Palma Norte for a couple of miles.

With the river on your left in the middle of nowhere, you'll see a sign reading "Rio Catarata" on your right. Park just before the bridge on the gravel shoulder on the river side of the road.

The short (five minutes) trail to the main falls begins at the sign. The trail leads down to a creek which divides. The left fork will take you to the main falls in three to five minutes.

The right fork of the stream leads you to another falls in ten minutes or so. This trail is a little trickier; at times you will be in chest–deep water. There is a very steep trail up the right side of these falls that surely leads to more falls, but I have not yet explored this trail.

Rio Puerto Nuevo Falls

INTRODUCTION

If a refreshing dip in a tropical swimming hole is on your wish list—as it doubtlessly will be in this scorching heat—a visit to Puerto Nuevo Falls is just what the doctor ordered. The falls are a little tougher to reach than Rio Catarata (40 minutes to an hour each way), but a swim in the pool there will more than compensate for your extra efforts.

The waterfall itself is pretty much a straight drop of approximately 120 feet over a wide rock face with little vegetation. Again, water levels drop sharply in the dry season, and the falls themselves are nothing to write home about after February 1.

The 30 by 60 foot pool of 78° F. (25.5° C.) water appears to stay full year-round, however, and that is the true drawing card of Rio Puerto Nuevo.

There are many flat sun-bathing rocks around the pool, but beware of rocks falling along the left bank: I missed getting my head bashed in by a matter of inches.

DIRECTIONS

Continuing south along the Pan-American Highway from the Rio Catarata, you will pass through a little "artist's town" called Curré.

The next little village you come to is called Puerto Nuevo. About 650 feet beyond kilometer post 235, there is a bridge over the Rio Puerto Nuevo.

You may park on the shoulder on the river side of the highway before the bridge; or if you look very closely, there is a tiny dirt road on your left about 280 feet before the bridge (fine for two-wheel drive cars). This leads to more private and shadier parking under the bridge.

The "trail" (such as it is) generally stays to the right bank in the beginning. After about 320 feet of hugging the right bank, it's best to veer off to the right along a "path" of rocks that parallels the main channel about 120 feet from the stream.

You'll arrive back at the stream at a small waterfall, best traversed on the left bank. A few minutes later, you'll come to a much nicer falls with a swimming pool. Climb the rocks on the left side, or cross the river and find the trail that cuts in on the right bank over large rocks. From the top of the second set of falls, it's stepping from stone to stone down the middle of the river for 10 to 15 minutes until you reach the main falls. (This last stretch could be tough going in the rainy season; use common sense.)

PALMA NORTE FALLS

INTRODUCTION

Although they're not the most awe-inspiring spectacle in Costa Rica, these little falls are certainly worth the easy 20-minute walk. My suggestion is to get some carry-out chow mein and egg rolls (Chinese tacos) from the Dragon Restaurant (It's the place just before the big bridge over the river in Palma Norte), and have a picnic here to take a break from the road.

The main waterfall is a cascade about 40 feet high, with a smaller stream entering from the right bank about halfway down, which creates an intersection of waterfalls. (This side stream dries up after mid-February.) The small pool below these falls is a perfect place for a soul-refreshing bath.

A second, smaller set of falls tumbles over the rocks a few meters downstream, and it, too, has a nice bathing pool. Between the two falls, there is an excellent picnic site for your Chinese food, and there's even room for a tent or two.

Above the main falls you'll find an almost unbroken chain of small intimate cataracts and warm bathing pools, any one of which could be on a tropical postcard.

DIRECTIONS

Continuing south on the Pan-American Highway from Puerto Nuevo, you will enter the outskirts of the town of Palma Norte. It's best to park at the transit police station on the left side of the road, then walk back (away from town) to the trailhead. The trailhead, which can be easy to miss, begins a few meters north of the "40 Kilometers-Per-Hour" sign on the edge of town.

The trail heads up into the mountains, with no apparent stream in sight. Initially the trail is steep and walking is hot, but it soon settles into a much easier and shaded level path.

At the fork in the trail, stay left on the main trail, which continues along the left bank of the stream. In about five minutes, another trail cuts off to the right toward the stream (there's a small campsite here). Stay to your left along the main trail and continue walking upstream. In just a couple of minutes, yet another trail cuts off to the right and leads to the two "main" waterfalls and bathing pools.

SAN PEDRILLO FALLS

INTRODUCTION

In my opinion, Corcovado National Park, which covers 110,000 acres (45,000 hectares) of the Osa Peninsula in extreme southwest Costa Rica, is the crown jewel of the country's park system. When a winter-weary gringo fantasizes about a tropical paradise, Corcovado is what he or she fantasizes about: mile after mile of deserted beaches, luxuriant rain forest, crystalline warm waters, flocks of giant scarlet macaws winging overhead. . . Well, you get the picture.

The south end of the park between Carate and Sirena is the most popular with tourists, and I certainly encourage you to find out why. One of the greatest weeks of my life was spent camping deep in the jungle along the banks of the pristine Rio Claro.

But no aficionado of tropical waterfalls can call his or her visit to Costa Rica complete without a visit to San Pedrillo at the north end of the park. One can reach San Pedrillo via a beautiful (but blisteringly hot) 11-hour trek from Sirena; I prefer the wet and wild (but pricey) boat ride from Sierpe, southwest of Palma Norte. However you arrive, you will find a remote outpost with rustic cabanas, beach camping, kitchen, and showers.

A half-hour's walk upriver from the ranger station is San Pedrillo Falls, your gateway to Corcovado. The falls are, once again, classic Costa Rican jungle cataracts. The main falls explode from the forest and spread out over a 60-foot rock wall to crash down on the rocks and logs below. You can get an unbelievable back massage in the warm pounding water, but a quieter bathing area awaits you at the bottom of the smaller set of lower falls.

San Pedrillo Falls are a pleasant and relaxing preview to the *real* attraction of north Corcovado—Playa Llorona Falls. Read on.

DIRECTIONS TO SAN PEDRILLO FALLS AND NORTH CORCOVADO

There are a few options in getting to the remote outpost of San Pedrillo at the northern entrance to Corcovado National Park. As mentioned, one method is to walk. First take a taxi from Puerto Jiminez to Carate, and walk to the ranger station at Sirena. The next day continue the beautiful, but grueling, journey to San Pedrillo. This route will mean two *hot* days of trekking along the beach, but the walk will be unforgettable, assuming you survive.

I prefer the wild boat ride from the little outpost of Sierpe, which can be reached by car or public bus from Palma Norte. Once in Sierpe, ask around for people heading out that way by boat. The price will start out high, but keep bargaining and whining, and you can cut it down. I promise you it will be one of the craziest boat trips of your life.

NOTE: Whichever way you go in Corcovado, be sure to call ahead and let them know you are coming. They *will* turn you away at the park entrance if you don't have your permits—a true bummer.

To reach San Pedrillo Falls from the ranger station, head south to a little building. The trail leads along the left bank of the river. In 200 feet or so, bear right, where the trail continues to lead you along the left river bank. The trail cuts across a steep ravine, which can get a little slippery. The trail soon arrives at the river. You need to work your way upstream the best you can from this point; there are occasional vestiges of a trail along the right bank, or you can slog straight up the middle. You should be at the falls in less than 30 minutes.

PLAYA LLORONA FALLS

INTRODUCTION

Playa Llorona Falls—the jewel of the crown jewels—is one of the most famous falls in the country. Ironically, it is also one of the least visited. Images of its pristine warm waters tumbling over a jungle-shrouded cliff onto a remote virgin tropical beach have graced the pages of countless books on Costa Rica, and stirred the wild savage in all of us who have seen the photos.

Looking at pretty picture books and dreaming is one thing, but sitting naked in the sand on a wild tropical beach at sunset while fresh water crashes around your body and ocean waves crash around the sea rocks in front of you is something else altogether—and it's an experience that remarkably few have enjoyed.

The trip to the top of the falls —where more jungle waterfalls and stupendous ocean views await you—has been enjoyed by even fewer. This is a shame, because it's not the impossible journey to get to Playa Llorona that some would have you believe. I'm not going to sit here and act like it's a Sunday morning stroll, either; it's not.

The key to visiting Llorona—and the hurdle that prevents most people from reaching the falls in the eleventh hour—is the tide. The falls can only be reached for an hour either side of extreme low tide (for example, if low tide were at noon, you could only reach them between 11:00 A.M. and 1:00 P.M.). It's a three-hour walk from San Pedrillo to the falls; it gets light at 6:00 A.M.; it gets dark at 6:00 P.M.; and you're not allowed to camp at Playa Llorona (although it's obvious by the well-developed campsite that many scoff at this ridiculous rule).

Boiling down all these parameters, here is the great secret: before you ever get to San Pedrillo, check the tide charts days ahead of time *to be sure low tide falls sometime between 9:00 A.M. and 4:00 P.M.* Then, simply begin your trek from San Pedillo three hours before low tide. The tide should be perfect when you arrive at the falls, and you should have ample time to get back home before dark.

If you want the maximum time at the falls and to return to San Pedrillo by dark, go on a day when low tide is scheduled to fall before 2:30 P.M. If you dare risk twenty lashes with a wet noodle for "illegal camping" on the beach in a national park, go whenever you feel like it.

The only really difficult and semi-dangerous part of the journey is getting around the rocky point at the falls. It is a six-hour round trip, however, and there are a few hills—so judge your own physical abilities and leave Grandma at home. Then go out and enjoy the quintessential Costa Rican waterfall experience!

DIRECTIONS

From San Pedrillo, head south across the river mouth. The trail begins about 280 feet upstream from where the river empties into the ocean. The trail cuts through the woods and soon comes back onto the beach. You must watch carefully for the trail as it dips in and out of the jungle and skirts rocky areas along the beach. Cross a good-sized creek (Rio Pargo, with a delicious freshwater swimming hole), and continue walking south along the beach. You will pass a landslide on your left.

Approximately 325 feet beyond the landslide, the beach (and trail, it seems) is lost entirely where a point of rocks juts out into the ocean. It is here that the trail turns sharply left, inland and uphill. Look for markers such as bottles hanging from trees, etc., to find the entrance into the forest.

For the next 90 minutes to two hours, the trail winds through the forest. You must traverse a few hills and tricky ravines, and cross a couple of muddy creeks, but the trail is fairly easy to follow because there are no other trails to confuse it with. The final descent to Playa Llorona is rather steep.

When you arrive at the beach (marked by a well-developed camping area), turn right and walk to the north end of the beach. A small set of falls empties onto the sand here—don't worry, these are not the falls (as some very disappointed tourists believe).

Assuming it is extreme low tide, continue northward up the beach around the sea rocks until you come to the falls, which cascade onto a tiny beach from the jungle 100 to 120 feet above. Keep an eye on the tide; when it turns, clear out or you will be stranded.

To reach the top of the falls, DO NOT attempt to scale the cliffs. Instead, take the trail back

toward San Pedrillo. Go back up and over the crest of the first hill, cross one tiny creek, and continue to a full-sized creek (Rio Llorona) approximately a half-hour from the beach below. This creek makes the falls.

Follow the creek straight down the middle as it winds its way through lush rain forest, skipping and gliding over several small cataracts with excellent bathing pools. In approximately 20 to 30 minutes, you'll arrive at the top of a postcard-perfect waterfall approximately 40 feet high, which must be negotiated—*very carefully*—along the left bank (facing downstream). There is an excellent bathing/shower pool at the bottom, and room for a tent on a small beach. I promise you will be totally alone in paradise.

The top of the main beach falls are about 160 feet downstream from these upper falls. Use *extreme caution* as you approach the rim of the drop, or the beautiful ocean view spread out before you may be the last of your life.

HATILLO FALLS

INTRODUCTION

I stumbled upon these lovely little falls while on a futile quest to find the elusive Terciopelo Waterfall (a beautiful falls that you can reach via horseback with guides from Dominical).

My disappointment at failing to find Terciopelo disappeared the moment my sweaty body dove into the warm-water jungle swimming hole at the bottom of this double falls. You can swim all the way behind the lower falls or enjoy an invigorating shower massage under the pulsating water.

Between the two small falls is a very private little diving hole surrounded by flat sunbathing rocks, scoring the falls a high Tarzan quotient.

What the cascades themselves lack in grandeur (both are less than 20 feet high) is more than compensated by the idyllic setting-a luxuriant jungle surrounded by tall trees. Topping it off is a gravel bar that provides a perfect campsite (bring an air mattress). Best of all, this quaint spot lies at the end of an easy 20-minute walk.

DIRECTIONS

Beginning in Dominical at the river bridge, head north along the coast road (toward Quepos) for 3.6 miles to the first big wooden bridge in the village of Hatillo. (Coming from Quepos, this will be the *second* major bridge in Hatillo, just beyond the Salon Chorotega bar). Park south of the bridge along the little side road.

This little side road heading upstream is the beginning of the trail. Arriving at the riverbank, pass through the gate, fork to your left, and continue up the right bank of the river. This footpath arrives at the river in a few meters, at which point you bear right onto a jeep trail. I negotiated this trail and river crossing in February in a two-wheel drive pickup truck with no problem, but I am not advocating you do the same.

Follow this little road past several houses on your left. At the point where the road swings uphill to the right, you will be facing straight ahead into a large field (there may or may not be a gate there). The trail may be a bit tricky to see, but you want to work your way toward the far right corner, generally hugging the bottom of the hillside on your right. This is a lot easier than it sounds—just follow your nose upstream; if you wind up in the river, just wade the rest of the way.

Cross the fence in the back corner of the field, and continue along the path that generally follows the right bank of the river. The trail will cross a small clearing, dip down to the left, and enter the forest along the right river bank.

The trail soon peters out at the river itself. From that point, it's an easy—and beautiful—ten-minute rock-hop upstream to the falls.

Pozo Azul (Blue Hole) Falls

INTRODUCTION

This series of four small cascades in a cool, shady dell provides the perfect respite for those a bit overcooked by the blistering sun on the beaches between Jaco and Manuel Antonio.

The cascades themselves, while pretty, are not dramatic—none of them measure more than 20 feet. The true drawing card of Pozo Azul is not the falls themselves, but the refreshing swimming holes at the bottom of each cataract. The third pool up is the nicest of all and has plenty of diving rocks.

After water levels recede a bit in January, a wonderful little sandy beach—perfect for camping and safe for kids—opens up at the very bottom pool (although you'll probably have some litter to clean up).

DIRECTIONS

Pozo Azul Falls lie in the hills above Parrita, a hot and dusty palm oil mill town about halfway between Manuel Antonio and Jaco. To find the falls, turn east (toward the mountains) 1 kilometer north of Parrita. Look for a sign pointing to Hacienda Tecal.

Follow this excellent road for 5.5 miles to a cemetery on your right and the Pulperia Los Piños on your left. Ignore this left turn, and continue about 975 feet to your next left turn, just before the bridge.

Turn left here and go 1 mile. Cross the bridge and park in front of a little store called Abastador Buen Precio.

The "trail" itself to the falls begins in mid-stream (in order to avoid a pesky land-crossing fee). After a few minutes of wading upstream, you will pick up a trail along the left bank. This trail crosses the stream once, and you will finish the easy 20-minute walk along the right bank.

NOTE: On the return trip, be sure to finish the last 650 feet or so mid-stream, or you will be charged a rather steep land-crossing fee at the house.

THE HOT SPRINGS OF COSTA RICA

With at least a dozen volcanoes in various states of sleeplessness, I am certain that Costa Rica is a mecca for hot springs. On a geological map of the Mt. Arenal Volcano area near Fortuna, I counted 37 hot springs. And that's just *one* volcano.

However, tracking down these little hidden pockets of Eden is a much tougher challenge than seeking out waterfalls. For one thing, the majority of the pools are tiny springs barely big enough to wet your little toe. They are only known to a handful of local villagers; if you don't happen to chance upon one of these people to ask, you're never going to know.

Furthermore, if you *do* discover an unknown hot spring, chances are that the spring is on private land. The laws regarding beaches and large streams are hazy enough in Costa Rica, but the general consensus is that the public has a right to use them as their own.

Not so with hot springs, apparently. Unless they are solidly within a national park, the private landowner has every legal right to bar the public from enjoying the springs. And you can bet that they exercise that right.

Originally, I had hoped to include a dozen hot springs in this book. After crossing out those with trespassing problems and those not big enough to sink your body into, I am left with only seven.

I would love to hear from those of you who have discovered others. Until then, I hope you enjoy this list.

RINCON DE LA VIEJA HOT SPRINGS

INTRODUCTION

Except for a mildly irritating olfactory hassle, Rincon de la Vieja Hot Springs (also known as Azafrules) is a wilderness hot-spring-lover's paradise. It is completely undeveloped, clothing optional (at least in my book), perched beside a cool, rushing mountain stream high in the cloud forest on a remote volcano. What else could one ask for?

The water bubbles out from the base of a white cliff at 108° F. (42° C.), but quickly cools to a more comfortable level as it circulates through the 20-foot diameter, knee-deep pool. Two smaller and cooler pools have been carved between the main pool and the river. If you really get overheated, the river is only steps away.

Azafrules is a hedonist's Nirvana any time of day, but the most magical time is after dark, particularly when a full moon is on the rise, painting the whole canyon a ghostly silver while you lie sipping your drink in the warm, bubbling cauldron.

The oak grove across the stream from the pools makes a beautiful campsite, but—horror upon horror—in 1992, the park service closed the area to camping; you will be chased out at sunset by the ranger.

If you want to enjoy the springs by moonlight and starlight, you need to camp in the parking area just outside of the park boundary (indicated by the split-rail fence 500 feet to the west of the pools). Otherwise, it's quite easy—and fun—to hike back to the lodge or campground beside the ranger station by the light of the moon.

DIRECTIONS

For directions to Rincon de la Vieja National Park, see the chapter on the national park itself. Beginning at the point where the road divides with one fork going to the ranger station and the other fork going toward the lodge, turn right toward the lodge, which is about a mile away.

From the lodge, the hot springs can be reached by a 3-mile jeep trail. I have successfully made this trip in a 1978 Toyota Corolla twice, but my rear-wheel drive Toyota pickup failed me—and damned near killed me in the process! So I don't advise driving unless you have four-wheel drive.

Driving or walking, the springs are easy to find. About a half mile to a mile from the lodge, the road splits; stay to your left here. You will cross a rushing stream full of rocks, then begin climbing a rather steep hill. Keep to your right, ignoring any small tracks bearing off to the left through tall grass.

The road continues downhill, crosses a muddy creek (where you are certain to get your car stuck if driving), and heads up one more steep hill before entering the forest. The jeep trail dead-ends in a parking area at the fenced boundary of the national park.

To reach the springs (which you can tell are very close by the sulfur smell), cross through the fence and follow the trail to the creek. While the springs are on the left bank, I find it easier to cross the creek downstream, walk through the oak grove on the right bank, and cross the stream again at the pools.

Rio Tabacon Hot Springs

INTRODUCTION

One of the greatest hot springs in Costa Rica is not simply a hot *spring*, but an entire hot-water *river* (90° F., 32° C.)— complete with rapids and small waterfalls.

The Rio Tabacon, 6.5 miles west of Fortuna on the road to Tillaran, bubbles out of the bowels of the famous Arenal Volcano and flows through thick cloud forest as it cools.

A couple of years ago, there was a well-developed tourist stop on the roadside, complete with swimming pool, man-made waterfall, etc. That side of the street has since been turned into a ritzy high-priced tourist resort, but we po' folks haven't been left out in the cold water.

A new, more natural, area is now open to the public just across the street and down-stream. It consists of a large grassy area that would be perfect for camping (not yet available) fronted by a 540-yard stretch of hot whitewater. Changing rooms are there, but the place isn't overdeveloped by any means.

At the same time, Rio Tabacon is far from wilderness. There is an entrance fee (about $2 in 1993), camping is prohib-ited, and the springs are not clothing-optional. The river caters to families (*tico* and tourist) out for a pleasant day trip. It's a perfect place for kids and Grandma. Be sure to grab some picnic goodies in Fortuna, how-ever, as there are no stores or restaurants there (at this point, anyway).

DIRECTIONS

Rio Tabacon is, at least, sim-ple to find. Head west on the main road out of Fortuna, toward Mt. Arenal National Park and Tillaran. The road crosses the river in about 10 minutes from downtown Fortuna.

You can't miss the huge resort on your left. The hot springs are just across the street; parking is plentiful and free. The walk to the river takes no more than two minutes down a gentle hill.

ARENAL HOT SPRINGS

INTRODUCTION

For those looking for a bit more of a wild experience than one can enjoy at the tame Tabacon Hot Springs, I would suggest a jaunt west just over the hill to the next creek. While not as splendid a spectacle as its big sister river, Arenal Hot Springs are a bit more private and relaxed. (Read: totally undeveloped, clothing-optional, and free. I get the sinking feeling this is all about to change, however. . .).

A good-sized, warm-water stream bubbles out of thick jungle into a small clearing, where someone has been kind enough to build a small "dam" of river rocks creating a couple of pools that can accommodate a dozen or more bodies easily.

The springs would be perfectly safe for families with small children, but the clientele there is generally young vagabond tourists from North America and Europe.

While there is not a lot of land around the springs to explore, there is room enough for a tent or two. If you plan to camp there, bring along some dry firewood, as there won't be any there.

DIRECTIONS

From Tabacon Hot Springs 6.5 miles west of Fortuna, continue driving or walking west on the main road toward the national park for a mile. You'll go up and over one small hill. There will be a small house on your left in a little jungle clearing just before you reach the springs. The path cuts off from the left side of the road on the west stream bank. It's an easy two-minute jaunt to the springs.

OROSI HOT SPRINGS

INTRODUCTION

Although it's about as far from a wilderness experience as you can get, Orosi Hot Springs offers a fun place to while away a few hours. Whatever there was of a natural hot spring has been tamed and channeled into three man-made concrete pools of varying size and temperature.

At 92.5° F. (35° C.), the baby pool is the warmest spot, but adults are discouraged from playing there. By the time the water has flowed into the main swimming pool, it is barely lukewarm.

Alongside the pools is a full-service restaurant and bar that offers a lovely view of the mountains and countryside. If you want to dip in the pools, there is a nominal charge (about $1 in 1993). Needless to say, nudity is prohibited, but there are changing rooms and safe lockers on-site.

DIRECTIONS

These well-known springs are in the middle of the old Colonial town of Orosi, southeast of Cartago on the way to Tapanti National Park.

From Cartago, take the road to Paraiso first, then continue on to Orosi. (There are plenty of buses and taxis running all day from Cartago.)

Once in Orosi, continue through the center of town, past the old church and soccer field, and follow the signs. The pools are at the end of a road to your right, a few blocks past the soccer field.

Los Patios Balneario Hot Springs

INTRODUCTION

Like its sister springs a mile down the road, Los Patios is anything but a wilderness experience. Again, any and all natural water has been channeled into man-made pools that are at least a little "classier" than Orosi Hot Springs. The sign advertises the warmest water, but I failed to notice any difference. The kids' wading pool is the only really warm water; the main pool cools to lukewarm rapidly.

DIRECTIONS

From the center of Orosi, pass the old church and the soccer fields, and continue past the road turning off to Orosi Hot Springs. About a half mile past the edge of town, on the main road heading toward Tapanti National Park, you can't miss the springs and restaurant on your left.

HERRADURA HOT SPRINGS

INTRODUCTION

A perfect example of a tiny isolated hot-water pool, Herradura Hot Springs is known only to a handful of local villagers. Located alongside a rushing mountain stream in the hills near Chirripo National Park, the springs are secluded and quiet, if a little small. The springs consist of one small pool, about knee-deep, with a sand and rock bottom. The pool is surrounded by huge granite boulders on the bank of a pretty mountain stream. There is room for three or four people to sit comfortably. As long as there are no *ticos* there, I consider the springs clothing-optional.

DIRECTIONS

Following the Pan–American Highway from San José and Cartago, continue south through the small city of San Isidro General. Go through the center of town, cross a bridge over a small river, and continue uphill.

At the crest of the first hill, a paved road enters from your left (marked by a sign to the Universidad Nacional). Turn left here, toward Rivas and Chirripó National Park. I *believe* there is public bus service along this road.

Follow this good paved road for about 5.5 miles. You will go through the village of Rivas. After the village, turn right onto the road leading to Chirripó National Park.

In about 5 miles, the road splits again; turn left here toward the Area Administrada. In another mile or so, after passing the ranger station and a couple of small bars, the road splits once more. Stay left here, toward the village of Herradura.

Approximately 325 feet past this split in the road, look carefully for a line of stones and an opening in the forest on your right. This indicates the beginning of the short trail to the hot springs. You must cross the small river to reach the pool. Aim for the tall tree and the huge rock on the far side of the stream, which indicates the spring.

RIVAS HOT SPRINGS

INTRODUCTION

Nestled in the hills on the west flank of Chirripo National Park, Rivas Hot Springs is a lovely and secluded little pool that offers a perfect escape from crowded tourist areas. The springs are not totally undiscovered or undeveloped, however—they are, in fact, quite popular with the locals.

The springs, just minutes down the same road from their kid sister, Herradura Hot Springs, consist of one small waist-deep pool surrounded by boulders. The pool has been artificially created with rocks by damming a small hot-water creek. There is room for ten or more people in the pool. Due to its popularity with the locals, I do not suggest nude bathing here.

DIRECTIONS

Starting from the trailhead to Herradura Hot Springs (see last chapter), continue up the same road for a half mile or so. You will see a small brown house on the left side of the road, and a clearing with a creek running through it on the right. Park here.

The trail begins at the yellow telephone pole on your right. Cross the footbridge over the river. When the trail splits, bear left toward the little house on the hill in front of you.

In front of this little house, bear right onto the trail that heads straight uphill. This trail is steep in places, but the huffing and puffing lasts no more than 15 minutes.

This trail arrives at a little house at the top of the hill, where you must pay a small fee (about 50 cents) to enter the springs. The trail continues behind the house; at the fork, bear left toward the sound of running water, and you will be at the springs in a couple of minutes.